Batsford Chess Library

OPENING
PLAY

Chris Ward

An Owl Book
Henry Holt and Company
New York

To my nephew and Godson Joel, a definite future GM!

Henry Holt and Company, Inc.
Publishers since 1866
115 West 18th Street
New York, New York 10011

Henry Holt® is a registered
trademark of Henry Holt and Company, Inc.

First published in the United States in 1994 by
Henry Holt and Company, Inc.
Published in Great Britain in 1994 by
B. T. Batsford Ltd.

Library of Congress Catalog Card Number: 94–76062

ISBN 0-8050-3579-6 (An Owl Book: pbk.)

First American Edition – 1994

Printed in the United Kingdom
All first editions are printed on acid-free paper. ∞

10   9   8   7   6   5   4   3   2   1

Editorial Panel: Mark Dvoretsky, John Nunn, Jon Speelman
General Adviser: Raymond Keene OBE
Editor: Graham Burgess

Contents

Preface

Welcome to a general openings book with a difference. In most texts you look up the opening and then find out the moves. Here it is the other way around! Play through the sections in each chapter and by the last page you will have the knowledge required to work out opening theory without having to learn it off by heart. The early stages of a chess game are of vital importance as the whole course of the game rests on the outcome of the initial skirmishes.

The layout of this book is very straightforward. I will tell you now though: if you wanted to know about Ruy Lopez being a sixteenth-century priest, then this is not for you. There is no beating about the bush here; chess is the topic and openings the speciality!

Take in the handy tips divulged and there is no doubt that you will be able to have complete confidence in your opening play!

Read on.

Chris Ward
Kent, July 1994

Symbols and Notation

For maximum ease of use, the chess moves in this book are displayed in full figurine algebraic notation.

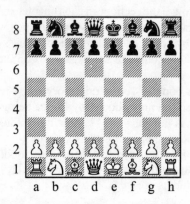

Thus a possible move for White here is 1 ♘g1-f3. The figurine shows which piece moves, while the numbers and letters indicate the squares the piece is moving between.

Otherwise very few symbols are used in this book. The following are the essential ones:

x	Capture
+	Check
!	Good move
?	Bad move
0-0	Castles kingside
0-0-0	Castles queenside
(16)	The current position is shown in Diagram 16

When a game is mentioned, the players' names are given in **bold,** with the player with the white pieces given first, before the hyphen. The place and in some cases the type of event is given in *italic*.

 Questions are indicated by a box containing 'Q'.

 Answers to these questions are indicated by a box containing 'A'.

1   Introducing Opening Play

1
W

As far as chess books go, the appeal of opening texts is obvious. Although endgame studies are instructive, as are entertaining tactical problems, there is only one guarantee in chess. As long as you are equipped with a full set, whether White or Black, you will always have the above position. Hence information in books like this must be useful so long as it is factually correct. Here of course you'll have to take my word for it!

Although I say 'books like this', in fact this one is a little different (I know, I'm sure most books say that!). Usually at the beginning there is a list of openings to be covered. A starting sequence of moves called an 'opening' often has a name (if that is the sequence is reasonable). Whilst this is usually the name of the inventor or leading pioneer (generally a

Grandmaster or International Master), it may also be the place where the variation or line was invented or most played. In addition it is possible that there might be some other reason behind its title. I would like to make the point that you should not let the name affect your choice of opening. Just because a player may consider himself to be patriotic, his own chess style may not be compatible with 1 c2-c4 (the 'English Opening')! Most sensible chess openings have a name, but in using the same logic as 'you can't tell a book by its cover' I am suggesting that you should select an opening because you are comfortable with the piece and pawn deployments that it entails. Having said this, I would advise against more suspicious sounding names like the 'Orangutan' and the 'Monkey's Bum'! (although by all means feel free to give them a fair trial!).

In this book I have attempted to supply the logic behind openings in order to justify their existence, before then giving the name. I do not pretend to have covered every single opening here although the reader will find at the end a reasonably sized index. There, reference will be made to any page that discussed the opening, but do not expect to be hit by reams upon reams of analysis. There may only be a simple concept or a useful titbit. Perhaps it would have been wiser to leave opening names out altogether although I do appreciate that, for example, one may wish to look up an opening that a future opponent may play, or perhaps so as to be able to purchase a more specific text later (e.g. *Winning with the Dragon*!).

Chapter 2 introduces the real basic general opening principles. However simple these may appear, the reader should bear in mind that the rules are at least a subconscious consideration for even the best of players. In Chapter 3 the sections get more advanced and similarly the accompanying questions get progressively tougher. With regard to the little quizzes, these are just to make sure that the reader is taking in the information. By all means cover up the page (i.e. the answers) in order to test yourself, or alternatively just gloss over them. In theory, Chapters 2 and 3 should supply the reader with enough handy hints to be able to produce some sensible opening moves of their own (whether previously documented or not). Talking about 'theory' we then move on in Chapters 4 and 5 to scrutinize some existing opening theory by using the lessons learnt in previous sections. Hopefully this succeeds

in demonstrating that the variations given in textbooks are derived by application of simple and logical chess rather than, as many seem to think, by pure Grandmaster inspiration.

We are taught that a game of chess can be split up into three parts: the opening, the middlegame, and the endgame. Where one stage finishes and another begins is a somewhat grey area. This means that although this book is dedicated to opening play, now and then I have encroached on the middlegame and occasionally have supplied the odd tip relevant to endings. Ideally the reader can master the opening sufficiently to win a pawn, fudge through the middlegame and then cruise to victory with this significant material plus in the endgame! Even if this master plan breaks down somewhere, it can't be bad to get off to a good start.

Generally textbook opening theory is based on GM or IM games. My intention in this book has been to show why these moves deserve a place in theory and why others don't. Hence bad opening moves are discussed along with methods of punishing them. The reader will observe that there is a lack of complete games (GM or otherwise) in this book. Rather than being afraid to step out of the jurisdiction of the 'opening', the simple reason is that I have only supplied all the moves of a game if I feel that it is relevant to the point that I am trying to make.

I will end here with the not surprising advice that, particularly in the opening, there is always something useful to do with a move. Therefore it follows that it is an advantage to play first. Thus especially at high levels, White is usually looking to get that little (or big!) edge, whereas Black is happy to equalize. So long as the reader pays attention to all the sections, this need not worry him, as he will always be aiming to play sensible and constructive moves, whichever side he is.

2 Back To Basics; Opening Guidelines

1) Put your pawns in the centre

Simple geometry tells us that the central squares of a chess board are d4, e4, d5 and e5. When phrases such as 'controlling the centre' crop up, then it is true that this group of four squares is of key importance. However when 'centralizing your pieces', it is not necessary actually to occupy these squares, so much as simply to watch over them. Hence the word 'centralizing' takes on a slightly more vague meaning (e.g. rooks on e1 and d1 are centralized). Placing your pawns in the centre couldn't be more straightforward. If White had a two move head-start, then **1 e2-e4** and **2 d2-d4** would be an excellent choice.

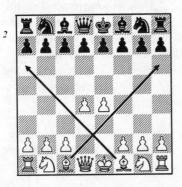

Note above how the 'centre pawns' now control some useful squares. In addition the white pieces now have far greater scope. The bishops in particular have freedom of movement, whilst the knights have a couple more options, and when ready even the queen can zap into action.

The precise importance of having central pawns is detailed later, but for the time being, suffice it to say that many openings are based on this concept alone.

1 e2-e4   e7-e5

1 d2-d4   d7-d5

With a simple symmetrical reply, Black prevents White from obtaining a central pawn domination.

Depicted below is the 'Sicilian Defence'. This extremely popular opening has been used by many of the world's top players, both past and present, the most notable of these being World Champion Garry Kasparov.

1 e2-e4   c7-c5

Q What is the initial aim of the Sicilian Defence and how could White attempt to finish

with both his d- and e-pawns in the centre?

A Black prepares to meet 2 d2-d4 with 2...c5xd4, eliminating the d-pawn for good. If White so desired, he could try the 'Sicilian 2 c3' variation with 2 c2-c3, attempting to obtain a 'big' centre with a later d2-d4.

2) Develop your pieces

There's no real point dwelling on this, as it is clearly a good idea. Possibly the best piece of advice that can be given is: look after your pieces and they will look after you!

Naturally of course they won't generally be of much use sitting at home. Hence one should bring them swiftly into action.

Q Are pawns pieces?

A The 'major' pieces are the queens and rooks. The 'minor' pieces are the knights and bishops. Pawns are simply pawns! Collectively the term 'material' is often used (to include pawns) and 'bits' is another, rather colloquial word for pieces.

3) Knights on the rim are dim!

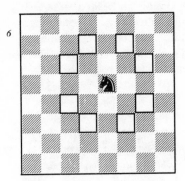

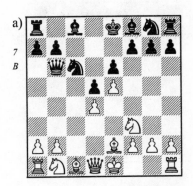

7 ... ♘g8-h6

A knight in the centre of the board controls eight rather juicy squares. Nudge this knight to the edge and its options are halved. Indeed approaching the corner it becomes severely restricted with a particularly sad knight monitoring just two squares. In the opening, as indeed the rest of the game, the idea is to give our pieces as much scope as possible. Hence the reader would do well to remember this little rhyme when placing his two knights.

I am often asked why it is that sometimes even World Champions place their knights on the rim where they are dim. The answer is obviously that they must have their reasons, most of which crop up in the following problems:

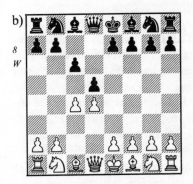

3 ♘b1-a3

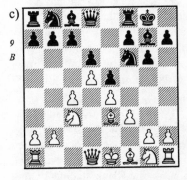

7 ... ♘f6-h5

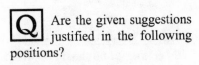

Are the given suggestions justified in the following positions?

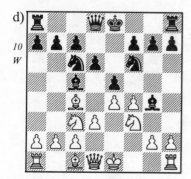

7 ♘c3-a4

|A| a) Yes. The g8-knight cannot move to the natural f6-square. However, it sees an excellent alternative at f5 and so aims to travel there via the rim.

b) No. It is extremely rare to see a good player's first move being a knight to the edge. Here the knight may protect the c4-pawn and be able to retreat to c2, but it has far better options from the more usual c3-square.

c) Yes. The knight has some ideas of eventually moving to a better location (f4 or perhaps g3). In addition it gets out of the way, opening up the possibilities of ...♕d8-h4+ and, better still, ...f7-f5.

d) Yes. White would like to castle kingside, but is unable to do so because of Black's dark-squared bishop. Thus this move would seek to eliminate Black's control along the a7-g1 diagonal – particularly the g1-square.

4) Knights before bishops

People have a habit of taking this rule a bit too literally, citing the 'Four Knights' opening as the best in existence:

1 e2-e4	e7-e5
2 ♘g1-f3	♘b8-c6
3 ♘b1-c3	♘g8-f6 *(11)*

Sure, this isn't a bad opening, but is it really necessary to bring out both knights before a bishop? To answer this, let us take a look at why this rule has come about. Take for example the following quite common position.

| 1 e2-e4 | d7-d6 |
| 2 d2-d4 | g7-g6 *(12)* |

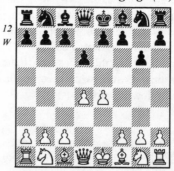

Of course White should not rule out the pawn moves 3 c2-c4 and 3

f2-f4, but if the choice boiled down to a bishop or a knight move, then I guess the third move candidates are ♘g1-f3, ♘b1-c3, ♗f1-e2, ♗f1-d3, ♗f1-c4, ♗c1-e3, and ♗c1-g5. This selection has automatically abandoned 3 ♗f1-b5+ (no prizes for checks!), 3 ♗c1-f4 (biting on the granite d6-pawn), and 3 ♗c1-d2 (fairly useless and blocking the queen's protection of the d4-pawn). As the white knights would be 'dim' on a3 and h3 and not very good on e2 and d2 then one thing is for sure: the bishops' possibilities are far greater. Since it is unclear which of these options are best at this stage (i.e probably Black's next few moves will have an influence), then for now it would seem more logical to play 3 ♘g1-f3 or 3 ♘b1-c3. This guideline therefore is really based around the simple concept described in Section 10.

Q Which of the two given moves should be preferred in the following positions?

a)
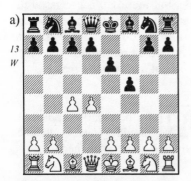

13 W

3 ♘g1-f3 or 3 ♗c1-f4

b)
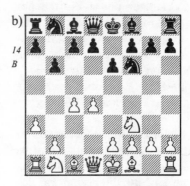

14 B

4...♘b8-c6 or 4...♗c8-b7

c)
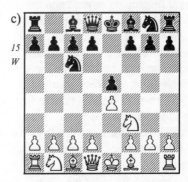

15 W

3 ♘b1-c3 or 3 ♗f1-c4

d)
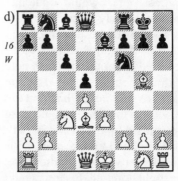

16 W

8 ♕d1-c2 or 8 ♘g1-f3

A a) 3 ♘g1-f3. It is far from clear that f4 is the best square for White's dark-squared bishop and so with 3 ♗c1-f4, White would be committing it way too soon. On the other hand, 3 ♘g1-f3 is a sensible developing move which keeps White's options more open.

b) 4...♗c8-b7. In fact in this position 4...♗c8-a6 is not out of the question, but it's more likely that with ...b7-b6, the bishop was destined for b7. Hence there is no point in hanging around and Black should immediately follow through with his plan. It is likely that the b8-knight will not fancy the c6-square at all and if d7 would eventually be a better location for it, then evidently 4...♘b8-c6 would be a mistake.

c) Either. This is very much a matter of taste. Some players would be suspicious of putting the bishop on c4 now, when it might not be best off there. In contrast, others would argue that this is definitely where they want the bishop and besides 3 ♘b1-c3 prevents a future plan of c2-c3 and d2-d4. Another point to note at this juncture is that if White wants to free his c1-bishop (and he will!), then he will need to move his d2-pawn. If he doesn't wish to play d2-d4, then d2-d3 is the alternative. In the latter case, the light-squared bishop would prefer to be outside the pawn chain. Hence either ♗f1-c4 or ♗f1-b5 will have to be played first.

d) Either. Another trick question. The reasons for 8 ♘g1-f3 are clear. White develops his last minor piece and prepares 9 0-0. Advocates of 8 ♕d1-c2 have a more technical answer. 8 ♕d1-c2 (threatening 9 ♗g5xf6 ♗e7xf6 10 ♗d3xh7+) avoids the pin that 8 ♘g1-f3 ♗c8-g4 would allow. In addition, White preserves the option of ♘g1-e2 instead of ♘g1-f3 and offers the possibility of 0-0-0.

5) Don't move one piece twice before moving others once

A common mistake that lots of beginners make is to send a piece or pawn out to battle to 'see what it can get' (including a promotion). Naturally they will lose it, but not be put off as 'there are plenty more where that came from!' I am not suggesting that the reader adopts that same tactic, but merely wish to issue the reminder that your pieces are an army. Hence one should not concentrate on one soldier too much without a very good reason.

Q In the next two positions, should White be tempted to 'go it alone' with the knight?

a)

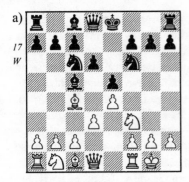

6 ♘f3-g5

b)

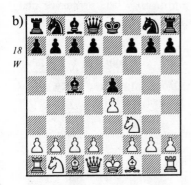

3 ♘f3xe5

A a) No. 6 ♘f3-g5 undoubtedly carries a big threat in 7 ♘g5xf7. However this would be easily parried by 6...0-0 and on a later ...h7-h6, the white knight will only have to retreat to f3 anyway. Hence White would be needlessly losing at least one tempo and this sort of selfish play wouldn't be taken well by White's undeveloped queenside!

b) Yes. A pawn is a pawn and this one is a centre pawn at that. After 1 e2-e4 e7-e5, White's 2 ♘g1-f3 both developed a piece and threatened 3 ♘f3xe5. 2...♝f8-c5 may develop a piece, but it doesn't deal with the problem at hand, and so should be punished.

6) Don't bring your queen out too early

Although there is no doubt that the queen is rather a handy piece, generally its role in the opening is more that of a deterrent. The problem is that it is *so* valuable, that when attacked by anything other than an enemy queen, it is not enough simply to defend it. So only too often when it is brought into play prematurely, it is soon forced to move. You will often hear that queens are very well placed in the centre of the board, having a somewhat lighthouse effect in looking around in all directions. However, a queen is only well placed there in the opening if it cannot be attacked by enemy pieces. Note also here the emphasis on pieces, when we compare two textbook openings.

a) 1 e2-e4   e7-e5
    2 d2-d4   e5xd4
    3 ♕d1xd4 *(19)*

(See diagram next page)

The Centre Game

b)   1 e2-e4   e7-e5
           2 ♘g1-f3   ♘b8-c6
           3 d2-d4   e5xd4
           4 ♘f3xd4 *(20)*

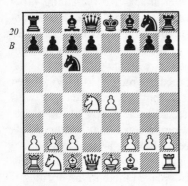

The Scotch

Q Which of these openings has the better reputation and why?

A The Scotch, as used by World Champion Garry Kasparov. Although (a) is not as bad as it looks, the opening has no takers at the highest levels. The

reason for this is clear. Although White retains a pawn in the centre, after 3...♘b8-c6, the white queen must retreat, giving Black time to gain a lead in development. In (b), Black can lure the white queen out with 4...♘c6xd4 5 ♕d1xd4. However this is not a good idea as she is placed well here. Of course Black could dislodge the queen with 5...c7-c5, but even if the queen simply returns home, 6 ♕d4-d1 *(21)*, this involves making three subtle, yet distinctive concessions:

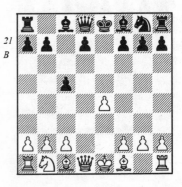

1) There is a very nice outpost for White on d5, just ripe for knight occupation.

2) Black's d7-pawn, even if it advances to d6, is a 'backward pawn'. There seems little chance of it ever advancing safely as far as d5.

3) Black's dark-squared bishop has just had its scope reduced, and in light of (2) above, its future prospects are somewhat bleak.

7) Castle early-ish!

OK, so the English in this guideline is a little ambiguous. The thing is that castling is definitely a good idea. Nevertheless one shouldn't lose sight of the reasons behind castling. These of course are to put the king into safety and to bring a rook into play.

In the opening one should always keep in mind where the king may go, this decision usually affecting where the pieces are developed. Particularly when the centre is open, it can be exceedingly dangerous not to castle and this is why we are often told to do so early on. Despite this, occasionally (often when the centre is blocked) it is possible to keep one's options open and delay castling. This may keep the opponent guessing as to which side (if any) the king will go, but note that a lot of care should be taken over such a decision.

Q In the following positions could White plan a sensible alternative to castling?

b)

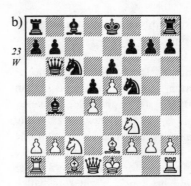

23
W

c)

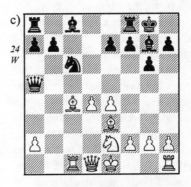

24
W

d)

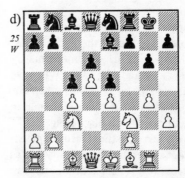

25
W

a)

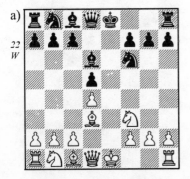

22
W

A a) No. The e-file is open and if White doesn't castle soon, Black surely will. Whoever's king stays in the middle will be subject to a rook check and will have to block it, thus walking into a pin.

b) Yes. In fact tactical reasons, namely losing the b- or the d-pawn, render anything other than 10 ♔e1-f1 unplayable. However this is quite satisfactory as White can soon advance his g-pawn one or two squares in order to create a safe haven for his king on g2. 'Castling by hand' is a phrase which refers to the manoeuvring of the king into a castled position over a few moves. When performing such an operation people often make the mistake of believing that they must finish with the exact castled set-up. In fact, so long as the two aims are achieved, then this is far from obligatory. With the king on g2, White's rook is better off on h1 than f1 anyway, so ♖h1-f1 (and then ♔g2-g1) are totally unnecessary.

c) Yes. 12 ♔e1-f1 is again a suitable response to the early check. The rook on h1 will momentarily look a bit sad, but White will have plans of h2-h4 and h4-h5 when this rook is very well placed to help in an attack on the black king.

d) Yes. Castling on the queenside is a very real possibility, but as the centre is blocked, it is not unlikely that White's own king will be just as safe in the middle. If White can keep a grip on the kingside (White's previous 9 ♖h1-g1 helping to dissuade Black from ...f7-f5), then he may choose to expand on the queenside with moves like ♖a1-b1, a2-a3 and b2-b4. Should he ever wish to connect his rooks then White could follow ♗f1-d3 with ♔e1-e2.

8) No unnecessary pawn moves

The white and black pawn formations, generally referred to as 'pawn structures', play a very important role in a game of chess. Particularly as the reader will later discover, the relative advancement of the pawns (especially the centre ones) determines the amount of breathing space a player has for his pieces. Nevertheless when weighing up the possibility of either an innocuous pawn move or some development (and remember pawns do not develop), then in the opening one should always plump for the latter.

Below is the very provocative Alekhine Defence, named like many openings after a famous Grandmaster Alexander Alekhine:

1 e2-e4   ♘g8-f6 *(26)*

26
W

With 1...♘g8-f6, Black initiates the Alekhine Defence. A piece is developed, though in contrast to the first guideline of this chapter, Black has not moved a pawn into the centre, nor indeed to control the centre. White has only two sensible candidate moves here. 2 d2-d3 blocks in the f1-bishop, whilst 2 ♗f1-d3 is pretty grim. In the opening bishops don't like just to defend pawns, and besides this move obstructs the d2-pawn which obstructs the c1-bishop, which in turn obstructs the a1-rook! We know that at this early stage queen moves cannot be seriously considered (these should generally be reserved for emergencies only) and a few words should be said about 2 f2-f3. The most obvious drawback of this very unnecessary pawn move is that it takes away White's kingside knights most natural spot. Perhaps worse still is that if Black follows up with 2...e7-e5 and then shortly with ...♗f8-c5, then White will have severe difficulty in castling kingside as his king is rather exposed.

2 ♘b1-c3, guarding against Black's threat of 2...♘f6xe4, and the text move are White's best options.

2 e4-e5   ♘f6-d5
3 c2-c4

Keeping the black knight on its toes, but hardly forced. 3 d2-d4 with the intention of meeting 3...d7-d6 with 4 c2-c4 or simply 4 ♘g1-f3 is eminently playable.

3 ...   ♘d5-b6
4 d2-d4   d7-d6

Black's knight has been chased around a little and finally with a free move, Black tackles a centre pawn. White's reply adds support to his centre and introduces the 'Four Pawns Attack' against the Alekhine Defence.

5 f2-f4 *(27)*

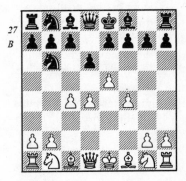

Q
Is five pawn moves in the first five moves over-doing things a little?

A
Yes, but the 'Four Pawns Attack' is a rare exception. Had Black have been bringing out his pieces while White was moving his pawns, then White may have found himself severely lacking in development by now. However three of Black's moves have been with the same knight (of course he was forced to break rule 5). Hence White can now develop

his pieces, safe in the knowledge that he has already built up a strong pawn centre.

9) Think of your rooks

Probably the biggest mistake that lower standard players make in the opening is not paying enough attention to their rooks. Of course they will laugh when they see absolute beginners attempting to develop their rooks as below.

1 h2-h4

'I think I'll swing my rook up to h3 and then along!'

1 ...   d7-d5

'I'm afraid my c8-bishop thinks otherwise!'

2 a2-a4

'Okay then, how about some action for the a1-rook?'

2 ...   e7-e5 *(28)*

'In your dreams!'

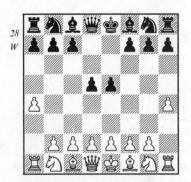

For White, this is *not* a good idea!

This is fair enough, but then they adopt an attitude at the other end of the spectrum that 'the rooks will have their day in the endgame'. Sure, rooks are excellent pieces in endings, but they can have an impact before then, and getting castled is simply not the 'be all and end all'.

If both sides maintain a solid eight pawn shell-type structure, then more often than not, the rooks end up sitting out the early stages of the game. Despite criticism of the previous illustrated example, one side may even try to zig-zag a rook into play. Swinging a rook into action along the third rank is indeed a common theme, but if not played under the right circumstances, it can go horribly wrong. By this I mean that with few available safe squares, a rook in front of its own pawns is prone to getting trapped.

Assuming that swinging up and along is not a valid option, then instead a player should seek to introduce one or both rooks into the game via a 'PAWN BREAK'. I have attributed capital letters to this because of its importance. Rooks offer five points each worth of 'fire-power' and how they are eventually going to be used should be as much a consideration as the development of the minor pieces. A 'pawn break' is just as it sounds. The challenging of an enemy pawn with one of your own, the intention being to create at least one open or half-open file. One should keep in mind these possibilities when selecting on which squares to develop pieces in the first place.

Only too often I see an opening start off approximately as follows:

1	e2-e4	e7-e5
2	♘g1-f3	♘b8-c6
3	♗f1-c4	♗f8-c5
4	♘b1-c3	d7-d6
5	d2-d3	♘g8-f6 *(29)*

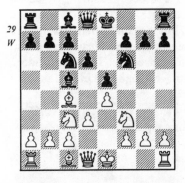

Both sides appear to be developing normally. White is now apparently worried by the prospect of 6 0-0 ♗c8-g4, with the intention of 7...♘c6-d4. Indeed, if Black did achieve this then White's kingside pawns would get shattered and his king would be in danger. Hence White guards against this threat.

6 h2-h3   h7-h6

Black anticipates the same problem!

7	0-0	0-0
8	♗c1-d2	♗c8-d7
9	♖f1-e1	

Right, so now all of the minor pieces are 'developed', it's time to start on the major ones.

9 ...   ♖a8-b8 *(30)*

Getting a little tired of the symmetry, Black diverges, seeking some action first for his queen's rook.

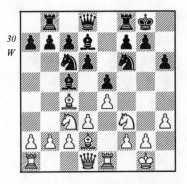

And the show goes on, but not for long! Both sides 'develop' their queens and rooks, but then they are stuck. Both players appear to have stuck to this chapter's previous guidelines, so what, if anything, have they done wrong?

Well, the first observation, which is discussed in more detail later, is the fact that simply 'moving' a piece isn't necessarily the same as 'developing' it. By moving their queens' bishops, both sides indeed connected their rooks, but this seems to be of little use here as they have nowhere useful to go. This then leads on nicely to the point that there is a lack of open or even half-open files. The reason for this of course is that neither side has attempted to make a 'pawn break'.

Just as many openings are based around trying to get pawns in the centre, the same can be said about those which try to obtain short- or long-term play for their rooks. We have already seen the 'Centre Game' and the 'Scotch'; a couple of others are given below:

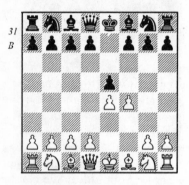

The King's Gambit

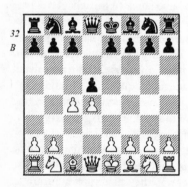

The Queen's Gambit

As the reader will later discover, the term 'Gambit' is a little misleading in the latter case. In addition, the former is a little more

risky since it appears to expose the white king. Nevertheless, the two openings have the common aim of attempting to get a second pawn in the centre, whilst creating some potential play for at least one rook along either the f- or c-file.

The 'Veresov' opening can be reached after **1 d2-d4 ♘g8-f6** preventing 2 e2-e4 **2 ♘b1-c3** once more preparing 3 e2-e4 **2...d7-d5** again thwarting White's plans. Alternatively, and with similar explanations, it can be reached via **1 d2-d4 d7-d5 2 ♘b1-c3 ♘g8-f6** *(33)*.

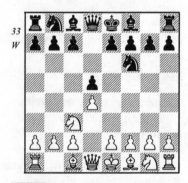

Q Why is it, do you think, that the Veresov Opening has few takers at the highest level?

A One evident difference between chess and snooker is that on move three here, White is unable to get his cue out and swerve the c2-pawn around the white knight and on to c4! His alternative pawn break, e2-e4, will be difficult to obtain since, in contrast to the Scotch Opening, there is no support for this break from the white queen. Of further hinderance to this plan will be Black's sensible development of his queen's bishop on f5. Meanwhile Black should have no intention of blocking his c7-pawn, with the obvious and good pawn break ...c7-c5 staring him right in the face.

10) Always make a move that you know you are going to play, before one that you are not sure about

Let us assume that in a given position you have three types of move worth considering:

1) One that you will definitely want to play.

2) One that you will probably want to play, but are not 100% sure of, as perhaps your opponent will do something to change your mind.

3) One that certainly warrants some consideration as – who knows? – it might possibly fit in with the scheme of things later on.

In which order of importance would you place the above?

Obviously your answer should be exactly as above: 1-2-3. Yet it is amazing how often this simple logic is not followed in actual games (and not only those involving beginners). This logic is what the rule 'knights before bishops' is surmised from, basically implying

that in positions of relative indifference, pieces of limited scope should be 'developed' before those of a greater scope. This is because something that your opponent may do, could in fact influence your decision regarding your choice of square allocation for a 'more options' piece.

With regard to this rule, do not get me wrong. Sometimes positions come along in which a move that you definitely will eventually want to play, can wait. I am also not trying to stifle any genius novelties or squash any good innovations born out of pure inspiration. What I do, however, advise is that the reader should take in the above and be very sure before venturing off the straight and narrow.

The guidelines given in this chapter are followed subconsciously by top players. I know that I, for one, certainly try to stick to these rules and would like to finish here with a game of mine in which I learnt a big lesson.

 Where did White go wrong in the following game?

Ward-Rausis
Le Touquet 1992

1	d2-d4	d7-d5
2	c2-c4	♝c8-f5 *(34)*

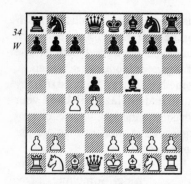

34
W

One could mix together a few bad starting moves and as an opening, it wouldn't have a name. This defence to White's Queen's Gambit is played by some reasonable players, but is in a big minority, in that it remains nameless – indeed the 'Rausis Variation' is most likely to become its accepted name. 2...♗c8-f5 is actually regarded as very anti-positional, although rather trappy. Black develops a piece. This piece is a bishop rather than a knight, but Black wants to get it outside the pawn chain before playing ...e7-e6, supporting the centre. The problem is that Black's last move does nothing to guard against the immediate 3 cxd5, which I suspect is White's best move. 3 ♘c3 is also very sensible, but here I chose the third theoretical option.

3 ♕d1-b3

Probably not the move I would have played if I hadn't known the theory! This early queen sortie exerts pressure on d5 and attacks the

no longer defended b7-pawn. In fact this move is often a refutation of an inaccurate ...♗c8-f5, although one should always be warned of the dangers involved in early pawn grabbing with a queen.

3 ...   e7-e5!?

Played without a care in the world. Not concerned about pawns, Black seeks quick development.

4 c4xd5   e5xd4
5 ♘g1-f3   ♗f8-c5!

Simply the best! Remarkably, the only textbook variation that I had seen, and rather foolishly memorized, was 5...♗f5-e4?! 6 ♘f3xd4 ♗e4xd5 7 ♕b3-e3+ ♕d8-e7 8 ♘b1-c3 ♘g8-f6 9 ♕e3xe7+ ♗f8xe7 10 ♗c1-g5 ♗c8-e6 11 e2-e4 c7-c6 12 ♘d4xe6 f7xe6 13 ♗f1-c4 e6-e5 14 ♔e1-e2. Then White would have a comfortable endgame advantage, but to take this line as gospel was, to say the very least, naïve. Certainly after the game, my opponent, who turned out to be rather an expert on this variation, found this rather amusing.

6 ♘f3xd4   ♗c5xd4
7 ♕b3-a4+   ♘b8-c6!

This is the beginning of a clever sequence of moves that highlights the disparity in the two sides' development.

8 d5xc6   b7-b5
9 ♕a4xb5   ♘g8-e7
10 e2-e3   ♖a8-b8
11 ♕b5-e2   0-0! *(35)*

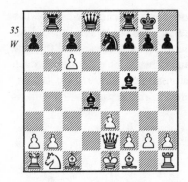

With a time limit of forty moves in two hours, I recall that at this point I had used well over an hour and my opponent just two minutes! This piece sacrifice was evidently part of his home preparation and I took stock of the position. I was naturally very disgusted with myself when I noticed that all of Black's pieces were now in play, whilst all I had to show for my first eleven moves (other than a couple of extra pawns which at this stage were not exactly promotion candidates!), was my queen stuck in front of my king – not a good place to be at the best of times.

Now 12 e3xd4 ♘e7xc6 leaves Black with tremendous compensation in view of moves like ...♘c6xd4(or-b4).

12 ♘b1-c3

A case of too little, too late, I'm afraid.

12 ...   ♘e7xc6
13 g2-g4?

Hoping for something like 13...♗f5-g6, when 14 ♗f1-g2 leaves White only one move away

from 0-0. Ironically 13 ♕e2-f3 would have been better, but by this time I had certainly talked myself out of yet another queen outing.

13 ...   ♗d4xc3+
14 b2xc3   ♗f5-e4
15 ♖g1-g1

If 15 f2-f3 then 15...♕d8-f6 attacks both f3 and c3.

15 ...   ♘c6-e5

Now things really begin to get painful with 16...♘e5-f3+ and 16...♘e5-d3+ both big threats. White prevents one, but not the other.

16 ♗f1-g2   ♘e5-d3+
17 ♔e1-f1   ♘d3xc1

Here **White resigned** as after 18 ♖a1xc1, 18...♗e4-d3 wins the white queen.

A It would be easier to look at where White went right! OK, so he placed a pawn in the centre and then made a strong and traditional pawn break (2 c2-c4). However after that things went rapidly downhill. He moved the same piece too many times before moving others once. To make matters worse this piece was the queen and castling early was clearly not possible with pieces stuck at home between the king and rooks!

Of course, if, after the early pawn raid, White had been able to consolidate, i.e. get developed and castled safely, then this extra material would eventually have won him the day. Nevertheless it appears that here, and far more often than not, given freedom of movement, it is the pieces and not the pawns that rule.

This loss made me wonder whether it was my shortest ever and for a while I was not too happy! However, we should all learn from our losses and this one taught me a lot – above all, even International Masters are not exempt from the basics.

3 Helpful Hints And General Information

11) The values of the pieces

No doubt this section heading will invoke a little confusion. Surely when we learn chess, we are taught:

Pawns   = 1 point each
Knights = 3 points each
Bishops = 3 points each
Rooks   = 5 points each
Queen   = 9 points

Am I about to suggest a different points scheme? Well, not exactly, although it should be noted that many teachers have proposed some changes. For example some recommend, and with good reason, that a bishop should be worth 3½ points and sensibly observe that a pawn should increase its value the closer it gets to promotion. I suppose that one should take these values as an average. Obviously a knight in the corner is not as valuable as an enemy one in the centre. However to reduce its 'points' value seems a bit harsh when, given time, it could vastly improve. Any given position will eventually be assessed on the scope of pieces, but first and foremost comes the 'material' situation and this of course refers to the scores on the doors in terms of the scale above. In other words, the value of each piece should really depend on what it is capable of at the time. As this is constantly changing, we have available a rough, but very useful guide.

Despite this, it is necessary to point out that with respect to piece and pawn inequalities, there are some differences between the opening/middlegame and the endgame. A very blatant example is illustrated below and is surprisingly common in novice games:

1 e2-e4	e7-e5
2 ♘g1-f3	♘b8-c6
3 ♗f1-c4	♗f8-c5
4 ♘b1-c3	♘g8-f6
5 ♘f3-g5?	

This move carries a big threat in ♘g5xf7. Nonetheless this breaks the rule of moving one piece twice before others once, and is easily dealt with.

5 ...	0-0
6 ♘g5xf7?	♖f8xf7
7 ♗c4xf7+	♚g8xf7 *(36)*

White has gained a rook and a pawn (6 pts), whilst in return Black has received a knight and a bishop (6 pts). Fair swap? No way!

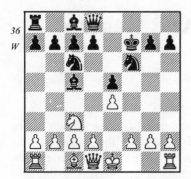

pawns, in the opening one should usually select the piece. A good example is the position below, which could easily be reached by incorrect play by White in the 'Two Knights Defence'.

In the very late endgame, with available open lines, a rook can, if teamed up with an outside passed pawn, prove to be a handful for two minor pieces (though rarely two bishops). However, the rest of the time (especially the opening, during which rooks are notorious lay-abouts), one should, given the choice, opt for the pieces. Indeed, one can generally throw one or two extra pawns into the bargain, and still remain on top. In the example above, it is ironic that it is White who has wasted moves in order to complete this unfavourable exchange. OK, so Black cannot castle, but his king can happily retreat to g8. Then, as White has no readily achievable pawn breaks, Black will eventually see more action for his one rook (down the f-file), than either of the opposing two rooks.

So far the reader has already seen that although one should place pawns in the centre, it is nevertheless pieces and not pawns that do the early work. Hence, given the choice of a piece or three

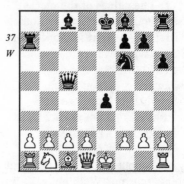

White has a very large queenside pawn majority which later in the game would no doubt be a real handful, but for the time being they pose no threat, and can offer no protection to the white king. Indeed when Black has completed his development, White will find himself swarmed by enemy pieces and is unlikely even to reach an endgame. Occasionally in the opening, provided there are active pieces as a complement, connected pawns can be a match for pieces. The 'Chigorin Defence' to the Queen's Gambit provides us with such an example:

   1 d2-d4   d7-d5
   2 c2-c4   ♘b8-c6

Just like 2...♗c8-f5, this move looks a little strange. Instead of solidly supporting his pawn centre, Black goes for dynamic piece play.

3 ♘b1-c3

Both 3 ♘g1-f3 and 3 c4xd5 are reasonable alternatives.

3 ...	**d5xc4**
4 d4-d5	**♘c6-a5**
5 ♕d1-a4+	

Knights on the rim are dim and this early queen move and follow-up seeks to embarrass the black knight due to its lack of flight squares.

5 ...	**c7-c6**
6 b2-b4	**b7-b5!**
7 ♕a4xa5	**♕d8xa5**
8 b4xa5	**b5-b4**
9 ♘c3-d1	**c6xd5** *(38)*

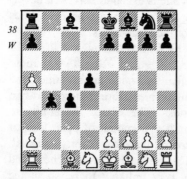

Although this is opening theory, it is debatable whether we are still in the opening. Black only has two pawns for the piece, although if need be, he could probably pick off White's a5-pawn. The point to note here is that Black's pawns (on the b-, c-, and d-files) are more menacing, in that they restrict White's pieces and are potential

promotion candidates. The position is very much in the balance.

There are of course other material inequalities. Often exchange sacrifices (rook for bishop or rook for knight) are made in certain openings. If two pawns are won as a result of such a sacrifice, then one may even be winning, even though ♗(or ♘) + 2 ♙'s = ♖ = 5 pts!

Two less common inequalities are reached in the following variation of the 'Pirc Defence'.

Q Who stands better in each of the following illustrated positions?

1 e2-e4	**d7-d6**
2 d2-d4	**♘g8-f6**
3 ♘b1-c3	**g7-g6**
4 ♗f1-c4	

White has a variety of sensible piece set-ups that he can adopt. As Black's next couple of moves (at least) are predictable, White should decide on his formation now, rather than taking things one move at a time.

4 ...	**♗f8-g7**
5 ♕d1-e2	**♘b8-c6**
6 e4-e5	

White deliberately delayed deploying his g1-knight in order to get the text move in.

6 ...   **♘c6xd4**

Black could decline the ensuing trade with 6...♘f6-g4.

7 e5xf6   **♘d4xe2**

8 f6xg7	🛒h8-g8
9 ♘g1xe2	🛒g8xg7
10 ♗c1-h6	🛒g7-g8
11 0-0-0 *(39)*	

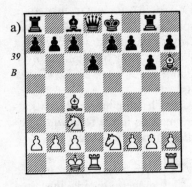

a)

39
B

deed positions are often a matter of taste. Some players are prepared to play this position with Black, although it is generally accepted to be better for White. The imbalance of queen for three minor pieces occasionally occurs. If there are no tactical problems for the three pieces, then his position is more likely to be preferred. He has three times the 'firepower'. This involves having both three times as much forking, pinning and skewering power and of course three times as much chance of being forked pinned and skewered! In this particular position, Black also has two extra pawns. However White is exceptionally well developed and there are no open lines for the black rooks.

11 ...	♗c8-e6
12 ♗c4xe6	f7xe6
13 ♘e2-f4	♛d8-d7
14 🛒h1-e1	e6-e5
15 🛒e1xe5	d6xe5
16 🛒d1xd7	♚e8xd7
17 ♘f4-d3 *(40)*	

b) White. Although 2 🛒's = 10 and ♘ + ♗ + ♘(or ♗) = 9, more often than not it appears that three minor pieces are preferred to two rooks. The key is the ability to limit the amount of open files or control the rooks' 'entry squares'. This is not a big problem here, and is very unlikely to be so in the opening.

12) The Fianchetto

With 1 g2-g3, we would see White going immediately for a fianchetto of his king's bishop. The long range power of bishops means that this one will safely rest on g2, whilst keeping an eye on the long diagonal from h1 to a8.

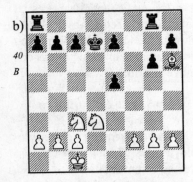

b)

40
B

A a) White. As I have said before, openings and in-

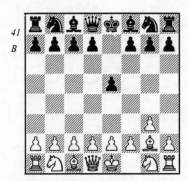

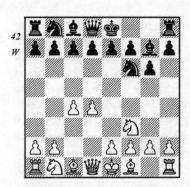

The g1-knight can still be moved to f3 as, although this temporarily blocks the bishop, it will lie dormant, ready to be unleashed by a knight move at any time.

Occasionally I hear remarks like 'I never fianchetto my bishops' or 'Fianchettoing just isn't for me'. The reason for these rather shallow comments is that fianchettoes are often associated with 'giving away the centre'. By this, and for example with the move 1 g2-g3, I mean that some players assume that by fianchettoing, one allows the opponent the chance to place his pawns nicely in the centre. Indeed, this is often the case, but there are plenty of times when fianchettoing can be played in conjunction with a good centre. Three subtly different examples of this are given below:

(See digram next column)

Black has already fianchettoed his king's bishop. Now White could play 4 ♘b1-c3, intending to follow up with 5 e2-e4.

Black could prevent this with 5...d7-d5 (the 'Grünfeld Defence') or allow it with 5...0-0 or 5...d7-d6 (the 'King's Indian Defence'). Another very sensible option for White is to keep the e2-e4 plan on ice for a while (possibly even for good) with 4 g2-g3.

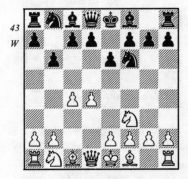

Black has just solved the problem of what to do with his c8-bishop in a very satisfactory manner with 3...b7-b6 (initiating the 'Queen's Indian Defence'). If White wants to get in e2-e4 then 4 ♘b1-c3 is an obvious candidate. This would then allow Black the chance to pin it with 4...♗b4 (not that this would be the end of the world!) and hence White could choose to guard against this with 4 a2-a3. Settling for e2-e3 means that White may have to decide where to put his c1-bishop. Such a decision need not be necessary now if White gets on with trying to castle (on the kingside as he knows that he is going to) with 4 g2-g3. This means that the light-squared bishops will be in line for a head-on collision, with the f3-knight determining when a trade can be offered.

44
W

White has played the Queen's Gambit, which was declined (by 2...e7-e6). Here 4 ♘b1-c3 appears the most natural move, or if White wants this knight on d2, then 4 ♗c1-g5 is also fine. However White has a third interesting alternative in 4 g2-g3 (the 'Catalan'). Not everyone's cup of tea, this opening removes the bishop from the diagonal where it defends the c4-pawn, to one where it can exert pressure on Black's queenside.

Note that should Black then play 4...d5xc4, White could regain the pawn immediately with 5 ♕d1-a4+ or continue with 5 ♗f1-g2 and have a later ♘f3-e5xc4 in mind.

There are a couple of drawbacks to the fianchetto. Firstly some holes are created. Take again the early kingside fianchetto 1 g2-g3. The square h3 has been weakened and there is a hole on g2. If the e2-pawn is advanced then there will be another weakness on f3 and there are often problems if the fianchettoed bishop is lost (particularly if the matching enemy bishop remains).

Secondly if one intends castling on the same side as a fianchetto takes place, then obviously the pawns around the king will have been moved. This can leave one a little susceptible to pawn storms, a common plan for White against the Sicilian Dragon, illustrated below.

1 e2-e4	c7-c5
2 ♘g1-f3	d7-d6
3 d2-d4	

With this move, White steers play into an 'Open' Sicilian. Black in effect gains an extra centre pawn and a half-open c-file (for later use of a rook or two). White obtains a centralized knight and has freedom of movement for all of his pieces.

| 3 ... | c5xd4 |
| 4 ♘f3xd4 | ♘g8-f6 |

5 ♘b1-c3   g7-g6

This move characterizes the sharpest variation of the Sicilian, the 'Dragon'. Black has no problems with his light-squared bishop as instead of blocking it with 5...e7-e6 (the Sicilian Scheveningen), he seeks to develop his bishop on g7.

6 ♗c1-e3

If White had intended to castle kingside, then 6 ♗f1-e2 or 6 ♗f1-c4 would have been more accurate. However 6 ♗f1-d3 is pointless since the bishop would have no future along this diagonal.

6 ...   ♗f8-g7

7 f2-f3

Laying the foundations for a future attack. This move also supports the centre and prevents a black piece materializing on g4.

7 ...   0-0

8 ♕d1-d2

Black's fianchettoed 'Dragon' bishop is often very powerful. This move prepares to trade off this key attacker and defender with a timely ♗e3-h6.

8 ...   ♘b8-c6

9 g2-g4 *(45)*

White intends to continue with moves like 0-0-0, h2-h4 and h4-h5. It is not so much the pawns that will be doing the attacking as the rook(s) that will act along the open file(s) that will inevitably be created. As White has wisely not moved any of his queenside pawns, a similar plan from Black would be far too slow. Instead Black's counter-attack should mainly involve pieces rather than pawns.

45
B

Q When fianchettoing, why are the g- and b-pawns moved just one square?

A The opening 1 b2-b4 is known as the 'Sokolsky', whilst the very rarely played 1 g2-g4 *(46)* seems to have had its name changed from the 'Tactical Grob' to the 'Killer Grob'.

46
B

These openings are conclusive proof that the knights' pawns can be moved two squares in order to fianchetto a bishop; the drawbacks are that the pawns are more vulnerable there. Above, for example, it appears likely that White will soon have to play h2-h3 to defend his g-pawn against &c8xg4. In addition, extra holes are created, such as those on f4 and h4, making things awkward should an enemy knight get there. The answer is that although fianchettoing can take place in this manner, it usually happens on the opposite side from where the king will castle. A very popular example of this is the 'Sicilian Najdorf':

1	e2-e4	c7-c5
2	&g1-f3	d7-d6
3	d2-d4	c5xd4
4	&f3xd4	&g8-f6
5	&b1-c3	a7-a6 *(47)*

One point behind this move is to prevent a white piece coming to b5, but the main idea is to prepare ...b7-b5. This expansion in itself would restrict White's queenside and create the potential threat of ...b5-b4. The c8-bishop will slide to b7, where it can exert pressure on White's e4-pawn and through to his kingside. Needless to say in this variation, it is quite unusual to see Black castle queenside.

13) The myth of doubled pawns

I'm afraid that only too often doubled pawns get bad press that isn't really warranted. 'Weak pawns' generally refers to isolated and backward pawns, though doubled pawns are occasionally and mistakenly included in this bracket. Admittedly doubled and isolated pawns can be pretty grim, but this assumes that the opponent has the resources to exploit the weaknesses. Don't forget that pawn structure is one thing, but piece play is a more over-riding factor.

The obvious disadvantage of having a set of doubled pawns is that there might no longer be an 'effective majority'. By this I mean that pieces aside, careful pawn blocking will mean that a majority will be thwarted with respect to getting a passed pawn. For example below, although facing a five to two majority (but with quadrupled c-pawns!), by playing ...c7-c6 rather than ...b7-b6, Black can ruin White's promotion prospects.

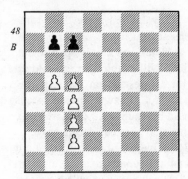

Of course, this is an exaggerated example and besides in the opening, where pawn promotion is very rarely an issue, there are two distinct advantages of doubled pawns:

1) Purely by definition, if one obtains doubled pawns, then a half-open file must have been created. This outlet can then sooner or later be used by at least one rook. Hence this may solve the problem of having to search for a suitable pawn break.

2) We are taught to 'recapture towards the centre', although like everything else this rule can be broken. The logic that implies that h2xg3 is usually preferable to f2xg3, partly involves minimizing the number of pawn islands. The other reason is that when transferred from h2 to g3, this pawn controls some useful squares. The same could be said of the f2-pawn, although by moving it, some control over the e3-square is lost. It is this concept of controlling squares (particularly in and around the

centre) that often makes doubled pawns quite desirable.

A favourable example of doubled pawns arises from the Anti-Sicilian 3 ♗b5+ variation:

    1 e2-e4   c7-c5
    2 ♘g1-f3   d7-d6
    3 ♗f1-b5+ ♗c8-d7

Both 3...♘b8-d7 and 3...♘b8-c6 are sensible alternatives.

    4 ♗b5xd7+ ♕d8xd7

Black could develop a minor piece with 4...♘b8xd7, but here chooses to recapture with the queen in order to post his queen's knight on the more active square c6.

    5 ♘b1-c3   ♘b8-c6
    6 c2-c4   ♘c6-e5?!

After, say, 6...♘g8-f6 7 d2-d4 c5xd4 8 ♘f3xd4 *(49)*, White, with his pawns on c4 and e4, has established a 'Maroczy Bind' as illustrated in the diagram below.

These 'binding' pawns attempt to restrict Black's play, by stopping him from expanding either on the queenside or in the centre. It could be argued that White has done well to trade off his light-squared bishop before placing his pawns on the light squares (c4 and e4). On the other hand, though, this bishop would help with this binding (particularly preventing ...b7-b5), and if Black still had his own light-squared bishop, he would be even more cramped.

The position above would not be the end of the world for Black. He could fianchetto his king's bishop and/or try to break free of his shackles with a later ...e7-e6 and ...d6-d5. However with the text move, Black moves the same piece twice (instead of others once) in order to stifle White's plans. Although not really justified, here he achieves his aim.

7 ♘f3xe5?   d6xe5 *(50)*

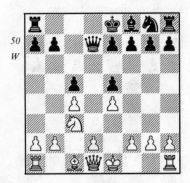

50
W

Black now has doubled e-pawns, is slightly behind in development, and has twice as many pawn islands as before (i.e. two rather than one!). However

two key factors more than compensate him:

1) Black has a half-open d-file, which will enable him to build up a lot of pressure on White's now backward d-pawn (major pieces could be doubled or even trebled). Note that this pawn can move to d3, but has no chance of making it to d4 or beyond.

2) Black has an excellent outpost on d4, but White doesn't have an equivalent one on d5 as ...e7-e6 will soon occur. Indeed Black's doubled pawns have control over the vital centre squares.

Do not get too carried away though. One must always consider the prospect of isolated pawns that may be left in the wake of a pawn-doubling process. Also it can be a problem if doubled pawns result in an exposed king. A common novice example and a junior favourite is illustrated below:

1	e2-e4	e7-e5
2	♘g1-f3	♘b8-c6
3	♗f1-c4	♘g8-f6
4	d2-d3	♗f8-c5
5	♘b1-c3	0-0?!
6	♗c1-g5	d7-d6
7	♘c3-d5	♗c8-d7 *(51)*

By now the reader should understand the inaccuracies that have been made in this game so far by both players. In case you are still unsure, then this simple 1 e2-e4 e7-e5 opening is discussed again in chapter 4.

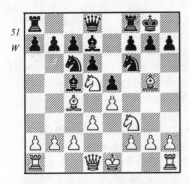

51
W

It is clear though that in the above position, White is very much on top. The pin on Black's f6-knight is very awkward and White has two ways of causing the black king severe distress. Firstly he can play 8 ♗g5xf6 and after 8...g7xf6, follow up with 9 ♕d1-d2, threatening ♕d2-h6 and ♘d5xf6+. Secondly he can play 8 ♘d5xf6+ g7xf6 9 ♗g5-h6. Then after 9...♖f8-e8, all White has to do is somehow get his queen to the g-file (e.g. ♘f3-h4-f5 and ♕d1-g4+) and *voilà*, checkmate!

Q If Black played 10...♘a5xb3 in the position below, which way should White recapture?

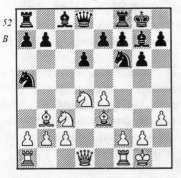

52
B

A 10 a2xb3. White recaptures towards the centre with a pawn that will now control a key square, c4. A common theme for Black in Sicilian positions (with a half-open c-file) is an exchange sacrifice (rook for knight) on c3. Besides weakening White's grip on the centre, the idea behind this is to shatter White's queenside pawns. After 10 a2xb3, should ...♖c8xc3 crop up, White's reply of b2xc3 will in fact leave him with no isolated pawns.

14) 'Classical' versus 'Hypermodern'

Most of the openings that we have seen so far involve the sensible concept of placing pawns directly in the centre or where they control the centre. This is the way that chess always used to be played and is known as the 'Classical' mode of play. Such openings include obvious symmetry such as 1 e2-e4 e7-e5 and 1 d2-d4 d7-d5, but extend to ones like the 'French Defence':

1 e2-e4   e7-e6

Black appears to be giving White a free run in the centre but ...

2 d2-d4   d7-d5 *(53)*

He immediately stakes his claim. However there is another style of chess ('Hypermodern') which involves letting your opponent do what he wants in the centre, with the intention of striking out there a little later.

The only way to achieve this without getting ridiculously cramped, is with a fianchetto. Two very common examples are illustrated below.

1 e2-e4	d7-d6
2 d2-d4	♘g8-f6
3 ♘b1-c3	g7-g6 (54)

The Pirc Defence

Black will fianchetto his bishop and then normally castle kingside. How he chooses to continue then depends to a large extent on how White develops. Earlier we saw White play 4 ♗f1-c4 here, and then 5 ♕d1-e2 (intending 6 e4-e5). 4 ♘g1-f3 and 4 f2-f4 are more

usual. Anyway Black's plans certainly include ...c7-c6 and ...b7-b5. However Black sooner or later seeks to play ...c7-c5 or ...e7-e5, possibly preparing the latter with ...♘b8-c6 or ...♗c8-g4.

1 d2-d4	♘g8-f6
2 c2-c4	g7-g6
3 ♘b1-c3	♗f8-g7
4 e2-e4	d7-d6 (55)

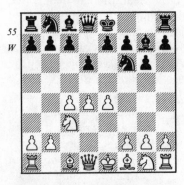

The King's Indian Defence

There is a clear likeness between this and the Pirc Defence. In fact the 'KID' is far more common in Grandmaster chess, although it is not surprising that there are some common themes. Whatever sensible set-up White adopts, Black at some stage aims for a ...c7-c5 or an ...e7-e5 pawn break.

A big idea behind Hypermodern openings is to try to provoke the opponent into over-reaching in the centre. A good example of this occurs in another sad practical encounter of my own:

Ward-Madl
London Natwest Masters 1991

1 c2-c4 *(56)*

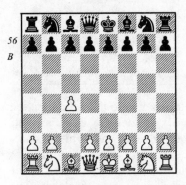

The 'English Opening'. The purpose of this is not to let the queen out, but to exert some pressure on the centre (already preventing 1...d7-d5). White could follow this up with a kingside, or even a queenside fianchetto. However in this game, White uses this as a foundation to put further pawns in the centre.

  1 ...   ♘g8-f6
  2 ♘b1-c3
Preparing 3 e2-e4.

  2 ...   c7-c5
  3 ♘g1-f3   g7-g6
  4 d2-d4

White is aiming to achieve a Maroczy Bind after, say, 4...c5xd4 5 ♘f3xd4 ♗f8-g7 6 e2-e4.

  4 ...   ♗f8-g7
  5 e2-e4

5 d4xc5 would be a short term gain only, in view of 5...♕d8-a5,

threatening both 6...♕a5xc5 and 6...♘f6-e4.

  5 ...   0-0
  6 e4-e5? *(57)*

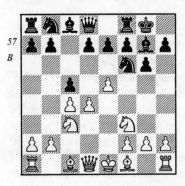

Very tempting, but also very bad. Black hasn't as yet been playing in the centre, but has made some very useful moves. As we will see, far preferable would be 6 ♗f1-e2 or 6 d4-d5 (this pawn would be safe here).

Q How should Black take advantage of this premature central pawn push?

A With 6...♘f6-g4!. Now White's currently big pawn centre is in big trouble and after just six moves, White is already objectively lost. The d4-pawn is still under threat from Black's c5-pawn, and when this is gone, there is no support for the e5-pawn. The key tactic which

White had missed was that after 7
h2-h3 c5xd4 8 ♕d1xd4, Black has
8...♘g4xe5! 9 ♘f3xe5 d7-d6.
Now Black is likely to finish a
pawn up, and it is she who will
have the centre pawns!

15) Bishops; The Good, the Bad, and the Ugly!

Although all bishops are val-
ued at three points, it is often
crystal clear that not all bishops
are equal. It seems sensible that a
bishop's relative worth should
depend on its scope. This should
theoretically tie in with the definition of a 'bad' bishop being one
which has its own pawns fixed on
the same colour as it. Note here
the word fixed. Some pawns may
temporarily hinder a bishop's
progress, but if they are flexible,
then they have the ability to
transfer themselves from light
squares to dark squares or vice
versa, so can avoid being a per-
manent obstruction.

To get even more technical, one
might also distinguish between
good 'bad' bishops and bad 'bad'
bishops, and likewise between
good 'good' bishops and bad
'good' bishops! A good 'bad'
bishop is generally one that has
managed to get outside its pawn
chain and a bad 'bad' bishop is
downright ugly! A simple distinc-
tion can be observed in the 'Advance Variation' (3 e4-e5) of the
French Defence:

58
B

According to the definition, the
'bad' bishops are Black's light-
squared one, and White's dark-
squared one, although in view of
the space situation, the former
looks worse than the latter. The
other two bishops are 'good', although if allowed to settle on d3, it
would be White's light-squared
bishop that is the tops. Generally
the white bishops are preferable
here, but this is not surprising in
view of his further advanced central pawns. Of course Black has
compensation for this in his super-
solid pawn structure, which appears impenetrable, yet contains
the flexibility to hassle White's
own pawn structure (with the
pawn breaks ...c7-c5 and ...f7-f6).

Many openings retain plans
which involve trying to trade off
their bad bishop for the opposing
good bishop. Indeed Black could
adopt such an idea immediately
above with 3...b7-b6. Rather than
fianchettoing the bishop uselessly
behind the d5-pawn, the point
would be to seek an exchange of

light-squared bishops with 4...♗c8-a6. Alternatively Black could temporarily continue to exert pressure on White's centre with 3...c7-c5 4 c2-c3 ♕d8-b6, but then after 5 ♘g1-f3, play 5...♗c8-d7 intending a future ...♗d7-b5.

The following queen's pawn defence is the 'Czech Benoni'.

1 d2-d4   ♘g8-f6
2 c2-c4   c7-c5
3 d4-d5   e7-e5

White could play 4 d5xe6? here, but this would merely provide Black with a handy half-open f-file, and a majority of centre pawns. Putting *and then keeping* a white pawn on d6 would throw a big spanner in Black's works, but this is impractical here as after 4 d5-d6?, 4...♕d8-b6 would mop it up.

4 ♘b1-c3   d7-d6
5 e2-e4   ♗f8-e7 *(59)*

59
W

[Q] Could you suggest to White a positional plan here involving trading bishops?

[A] Yes, starting with 6 g2-g3. White could then follow up with 7 ♗f1-h3, or better still prepare this bad-for-good exchanging process after 6...0-0, with 7 h2-h4. This would leave any recapturing white piece safer on h3, and prevent Black from returning the favour with ...♘f6-e8 and ...♗e7-g5.

16) Open and Closed positions

Whether a position is 'Open' or 'Closed' (or indeed semi-open or semi-closed!), is entirely down to the pawn structure. The more blockages (i.e. fixed set of pawns) there are, the more closed a position is. Closed positions notoriously involve clever timing of any remaining pawn breaks, and subtle manoeuvring of knights to good squares. Often people are heard saying that they don't like closed positions. Indeed openings can usually be specially selected so as to maintain an open game, but it does pay dividends to have practice in, and thus be prepared to play, more closed positions.

A good comparison can be made by observing two similar-looking, but very different openings.

a)   1 d2-d4   ♘g8-f6
      2 c2-c4   g7-g6
      3 ♘b1-c3   ♗f8-g7
      4 e2-e4   d7-d6
      5 f2-f3

This is known as the 'Sämisch' variation against Black's King's

Indian Defence. White supports his e4-pawn and guards against an annoying ...♘f6-g4, should his c1-bishop want to settle on the very sensible e3-square. In addition White has his pawns nicely positioned to start an attack, if so desired, with g2-g4, h2-h4-h5. Often one might need to develop completely and get castled before embarking on such a plan, but if the centre were to become blocked, then the king might be fairly safe in the middle, and so the ball could start rolling ahead of schedule.

5 ...   0-0
6 ♗c1-e3

Tucked in nicely and supporting the centre. 6 ♗c1-f4? would see this bishop just biting on granite, but 6 ♗c1-g5 applying some latent pressure to the e7-pawn (and setting up a pin should it move), is certainly playable.

6 ...   e7-e5

Immediately striking back in the centre. Here in fact Black has numerous possibilities. Black could similarly play 6...c7-c5 (evidently offering a pawn sacrifice) or prepare this move with 6...♘b8-d7. Alternatively he could, for the time being, ignore the centre, say with 6...a7-a6 (or 6...c7-c6), intending to play for ...b7-b5. 6...♘b8-c6 is also very reasonable, keeping both the ...e7-e5 and ...b7-b5 pawn breaks in the melting pot.

7 d4-d5 *(60)*

By no means forced, since 7 ♘g1-e2 is perfectly feasible.

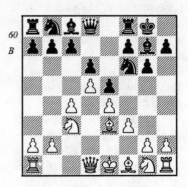

b)   1 d2-d4   ♘g8-f6
2 c2-c4   g6-g6
3 ♘b1-c3   d7-d5
4 c4xd5

Against this 'Grünfeld Defence', White here opts for the 'Exchange Variation'. Not necessarily better, but rather less committal are 4 ♘g1-f3 and 4 ♗c1-g5.

4 ...   ♘f6xd5
5 e2-e4   ♘d5xc3
6 b2xc3   ♗f8-g7 *(61)*

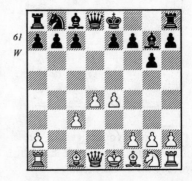

Q Describe the type of position reached in both (a) and (b).

A a) Closed. No pawns have been exchanged and this leaves both sides searching for a pawn break, to bring a rook or two to life. Often, with fixed pawns, the direction in which the pawns lean, gives you a good idea of where to aim your next pawn (in a pawn chain) and hence which side of the board to concentrate your efforts. Here for example Black has pawns on c7, d6 and e5. The next logical step would be to get one on f4. He can at least start by getting in ...f7-f5 and this explains why 7...♘f6-e8, and 7...♘f6-h5 are common here. White's logical next step is to open the c-file, by eventually attempting to play c4-c5.

Note that it is very possible for both players to go 'against the grain'. Here 7...c7-c5 and 7...c7-c6 have both been played by strong players. White, for his part, may prefer to delay c4-c5, and if he gets the chance, aim to restrict Black with g2-g4, even with the intention of starting a kingside attack.

b) Open. There are already two half-open files and however White chooses to develop, Black is likely to play ...c7-c5 shortly, which will ultimately create an open c-file. At present White has a very nice pawn centre, but he must tread carefully as Black will aim to de-stroy it. After an almost inevitable ...c5xd4 and c3xd4, it will also be noticeable that, while White will retain an extra centre pawn, Black will have a queenside pawn majority. This will become more relevant should an endgame arise. The distinguishing feature of open positions is the freedom of movement that the pieces have. This is quite true here, even of the black pieces that have the white centre pawns to contend with.

17) The difference between moving a piece and developing a piece

It is fairly obvious, and indeed was stressed in Chapter 2, that in general you need your pieces 'out' in order for them to do anything useful. There it was also mentioned that you should treat your pieces as an army and hence try to get them coordinated. Nevertheless players often make the mistake of moving all of their pieces once just for the sake of doing so.

With a hypothetical example of Black playing very badly against the Advance Variation of the French Defence, we see below for the first time in this book, the 'Greek Gift'.

1	e2-e4	e7-e6
2	d2-d4	d7-d5
3	e4-e5	♗f8-b4+?

If Black isn't aware of the pawn break 3...c7-c5, then in fact he is already in deep trouble. The flawed logic behind this move is that Black's kingside minor pieces would otherwise be fighting over the e7-square. Of course with the centre blocked, it is actually possible for him to delay the deployment of these pieces until something good comes along.

4 c2-c3

White could also happily play 4 ♗c1-d2 offering a trade of bad for good bishop.

4 ...	**♗b4-a5**
5 ♘g1-f3	**♘g8-e7**
6 ♗f1-d3	**♘b8-c6**
7 0-0	**♗c8-d7**
8 ♖f1-e1	

White could greedily gain more space on the queenside with 8 b2-b4, but assuming he was going to develop a piece, was the rook the right choice? Well, it was certainly a very reasonable one as amongst other uses it may even participate in an attack via the third rank. Remember that White's fixed pawns 'lean' towards the kingside and so it is logical for him to concentrate his efforts there. The b1-knight could have moved to d2, with the intention of hopping to b3 and then c5, but another option is to send it to g3 via f1. The rook move facilitates this possibility.

More common amongst novices would have been something like 8 ♗c1-f4. The idea behind this would have been to allow the non-bishop-blocking-in 9 ♘b1-d2. Then White would be quite happy as he has moved all of his minor pieces. The reality of the situation is that the bishop serves no more purpose on f4 than it does on c1 (in fact it might even get in the way). Bearing in mind the lack of open and half-open files, connecting the rooks is of relatively little consequence and as it was far from clear (in fact unlikely) that the bishop wants to go to f4, then moving this piece is effectively wasting a move.

8 ...   0-0 *(62)*

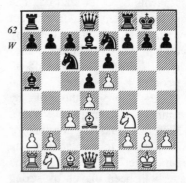

62
W

Black has moved all of his minor pieces and is now castled. One might argue that strictly speaking he is ahead in development, but are his pieces really doing anything useful? The answer of 'No' is delivered with White's stunning next move.

9 ♗d3xh7+!

The 'Greek Gift' sacrifice to drag Black's king into the open. Declining this sacrifice with 9...♔g8-h8 is of little help as White could follow up with ♘f3-

g5 and ♕d1-h5 anyway (before or after retreating the h7-bishop).

9 ...   ♚g8xh7
10 ♘f3-g5+   ♚h7-g8

Bringing the king further out with 10...♚h7-g6 is well met by the quiet, but very threatening 11 ♕d1-g4. 10...♚h7-h8 invites the two move finish 11 ♕d1-h5+ ♚h8-g8 12 ♕h5-h7 mate, whilst even the so called 'undeveloped' bishop on c1 joins in after 10...♚h7-h6 11 ♘g5xf7(or e6)+.

11 ♕d1-h5   ♖f8-e8 *(63)*

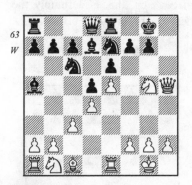

Q The black king is on the ropes, but how should White finish him off?

A White has more than one way of winning this position. The easiest way appears to be by introducing his rook with 12 ♕h5xf7+ ♚g8-h8 13 ♖e1-e3 ♘e7-f5 14 ♖e3-h3+ ♘f5-h6 15 ♖h3xh6+ g7xf6 16 ♕f7-h7 mate. However in fact using the rook may be deemed as surplus to requirements in view of 12 ♕h5-h7+

♚g8-f8 13 ♕h7-h8+ ♘e7-g8 14 ♘g5-h7+ ♚f8-e7 15 ♗c1-g5+, when 15...♘g8-f6 will lose a lot of material and 15...f7-f6 allows 16 ♕h8xg7 mate. I myself would prefer the former, which fully justifies White's 8th move.

18) The importance of centre pawns

Once a centre pawn makes it to the fifth rank, it really encroaches upon enemy territory, immediately taking away a resting place of an opponent's knight. Once the opposition's pieces have been forced back, it is possible to bring forward ones own under the cover of the pawns.

A good example of this is demonstrated in the following nice game between a promising junior (with minimal help from his coach!) and a metal box:

T.Jarrett-His Chess Computer
Maidstone 1992

1 d2-d4   d7-d5
2 c2-c4   c6-c6 *(64)*

Again we see the Queen's Gambit, but here the machine employs the 'Slav Defence'.

3 ♘b1-c3   ♞g8-f6
4 c4xd5

The other candidate moves in this position are 4 ♘g1-f3 and 4 e2-e3. Note the latter seems a little illogical in that it blocks in the c1-bishop. It may appear that Black could instead bring out his c8-bishop before playing ...e7-e6, but in fact after 4...♝c8-f5, 5 cxd5 cxd5 6 ♕d1-b3 is quite difficult to deal with – the best reply is probably 6...♝f5-c8(!).

4 ...   ♞f6xd5?!

Showing remarkably poor logic for a computer. The point behind 2...c7-c6 is to support the centre and for the time being at least, guarantee that a black pawn would stay there.

5 e2-e4

Never look a gift horse in the mouth (unless it's Trojan!).

5 ...   ♞d5xc3
6 b2xc3   e7-e6

Adopting a solid, but very passive pawn structure.

7 ♘g1-f3   ♝f8-d6?

A decision which must often be made in the opening is whether a bishop should go to e7 or d6 (if it's black) or e2 or d3 (if it's white). In order to arrive at the correct choice, one should consider how active its teammates are. Clearly, here and generally, the black bishop is in a more attacking post on d6. However as Black's other pieces are nowhere to be seen, this aggressive deployment is wrong. In fact the bishop is now forced back to its best (defensive) square.

Black should at least be looking to pressurize White's strong centre quickly with his c-pawn, but having already played ...c7-c6, the computer seems to have difficulty in swallowing its pride.

8 e4-e5   ♝d6-e7
9 ♝f1-d3

In contrast to Black, with plenty of back-up, this is definitely the best square for the f1-bishop.

9 ...   ♞b8-d7
10 0-0   0-0 *(65)*

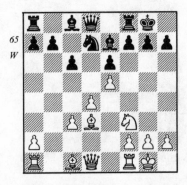

65
W

The reader should note here that Black certainly made the correct retreat on his 8th move. Were this bishop now on c7 instead of e7, then White could come straight to the point with 11 ♝d3xh7+!. The e5-pawn then has the key role of keeping a knight from the f6-square. Clearly the e7-bishop now prohibits this continuation, but another titbit is that if White could now substitute 10 0-0 for 10 h2-h4, then the Greek Gift would be on again as after 11 ♗h3xh7+ ♔g8xh7 12 ♘f3-g5+ ♗e7xg5+ 13 h4xg5+ means that the h1-rook replaces the knight as the white queen's partner in crime.

11 ♕d1-e2!
Preparing to bring the queen into action. From the last section, one should realize that the fate of the c1-bishop is far from decided, and so there is no point moving it yet.

11 ...	**♘d7-b6**
12 ♕e2-e4	**g7-g6**
13 ♗c1-h6	**♖f8-e8**
14 h2-h4!	

White sets about weakening the pawn structure around the black king.

14 ...	**♕d8-d5**
15 ♕e4-g4	

Naturally White avoids the queen trade and at the same time unleashes the d3-bishop. Note how the e5-pawn (supported by the d4-pawn and in turn by the c3-pawn) prevents Black's pieces from aiding in the defence of their king.

15 ...	**♗c8-d7**
16 h4-h5 *(66)*	

Now there is a threat. White has up his sleeve 17 h5xg6 h7xg6 18 ♗d3xg6 f7xg6 19 ♕g4xg6+ ♔g8-h8 20 ♕g6-g7 mate. Black anticipates this, but is visibly struggling.

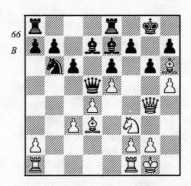

66
B

16 ...	**♔g8-h8**
17 ♘f3-g5	

Now all of White's pieces are getting in on the act. If Black now plays 17...♔h8-g8, then 18 ♘g5xf7 is just one way of eliminating Black's flimsy cover.

17 ...	**♗e7xg5**

A horrible move to have to play. In relinquishing his only defender, Black leaves the dark-squared holes around his king at White's mercy.

18 ♕g4xg5	**♔h8-g8**
19 ♕g5-f6	**1-0**

There is no defence to the mate on g7.

Q Did Black go tactically wrong in this game?

A Although technology is progressing at an impressive rate, it was never characteristic of computers to make tactical errors. This is indeed true of this game as well. Black is indeed no material down in the final position, and never looked like being so. It is therefore clear that one cannot avoid losing just by not giving pieces away. Black's positional play here was very dubious despite its having 'developed' all but one of its pieces. The point is that with poor positional play, tactical concessions are inevitable (e.g. to avoid mate in one above, Black must play 19...♛d5xe5). The answer to the question is no, and in fact earlier in this game Black could have put up a better fight by conceding the exchange. As this lost material though, it is doubtful that with this particular model, this was a serious consideration.

19) Space; The Final Frontier!

This topic is obviously related to the last, as it is very clear that the player with the advanced centre pawns tends to have a space advantage. The question really is: what is the purpose of a space advantage? Of course it isn't necessarily money in the bank in terms of extra material, but it is often a step in the direction of obtaining this, or indeed checkmate. The logic behind this is that if sufficiently restricted, one might concede material (e.g. a piece for a couple of cramping pawns) in order to obtain more freedom of movement for the other pieces.

The key advantage of having more space is that one's pieces have more mobility. In contrast to the opponent, one has the ability to transfer one's own pieces easily from one side of the board to the other. In my view an excellent example of utilizing this advantage is a game involving a legendary World Champion (and, rumour has it, cable television repair man!), Bobby Fischer.

Fischer-Gheorghiu
Buenos Aires 1970

1 e2-e4	e7-e5
2 ♘g1-f3	♞g8-f6 *(67)*

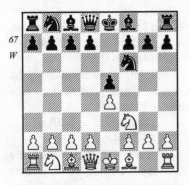

The Petroff Defence

This opening is often played accidentally by beginners, with the disastrous continuation 3 ♘f3xe5 ♞f6xe4? 4 ♕d1-e2 ♞e4-f6? 5 ♘e5-c6+, winning the black queen.

3 ♘f3xe5

Probably the best continuation, with 3 d2-d4 running a close second.

3 ...	d7-d6

4 ♘e5-f3   ♞f6xe4
5 d2-d4

It is often suggested that if White is happy with a draw, then he should play 5 ♕d1-e2 ♛d8-e7 6 d2-d3 ♞g8-f6. Interestingly enough, Fischer played exactly this in the United States Championship ten years earlier, and after 7 ♗c1-g5, converted his extremely minimal advantage into a win.

5 ...   ♝f8-e7
6 ♗f1-d3   ♞e4-f6?!

Altogether too passive really. Grandmasters of today would prefer to stake a claim in the centre with ...d7-d5 either now or on the last move. Then White should eventually try to dislodge the black knight with a timely c2-c4 thrust.

7 h2-h3!

Showing superb judgement. Instead of castling or developing another piece, White removes the g4-square from Black's light-squared bishop. As you will soon see, this leaves its options very limited. Hence this is definitely not categorized as an unnecessary pawn move.

7 ...   0-0
8 0-0   ♖f8-e8
9 c2-c4

Using the c-pawn to wisely gain more space in the centre before playing ♘b1-c3.

9 ...   ♞b8-c6
10 ♘b1-c3 *(68)*

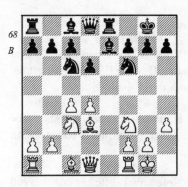

Already we can see that although Black has no apparent weaknesses and a seemingly solid pawn structure, in fact he is quite cramped. There is an open e-file and like White, Black would like to get his major pieces on it. However, bearing in mind the amount of safe squares available to the c8-bishop (i.e. one on d7), he would have to be a contortionist in order to achieve this aim.

10 ...   h7-h6
11 ♖f1-e1   ♝e7-f8
12 ♖e1xe8

Black is desperate to exchange pieces so as to alleviate his worries of claustrophobia. Wherever possible, if not compromising his position, White should avoid straight swaps. On this occasion Fischer obliges, but only in the knowledge that the e-file will soon be his.

12 ...   ♛d8xe8
13 ♗c1-f4

'Moving' the bishop so as to allow the a1-rook to enter the action.

13 ...   ♝c8-d7
14 ♕d1-d2

Now Black's problems really begin. How on Earth can he get his rook to the e-file?

14 ...   ♕e8-c8

Hoping to exchange bishops, or at least gain more room, with 15...♝d7-f5.

15 d4-d5

Note how White has only played this move now he knows that ...♞c6-e5 is not an option. Hence the e5-square is unavailable to Black, whilst the d4-square becomes ripe for White's occupation.

15 ...   ♞c6-b4
16 ♞c3-e4

Again, White wants to avoid 'fair' swaps and this is a clever way of doing so. Now 16...♞b4xd3 17 ♞e4xf6+ leaves the pawns around Black's king horribly shattered.

16 ...   ♞f6xe4
17 ♝d3xe4

White looks upon this last exchange as having removed a key defender. The fact that the b4-knight is *en prise* means that Black has no time for 17...♝d7-f5.

17 ...   ♞b4-a6
18 ♞f3-d4   ♞a6-c5
19 ♝e4-c2 *(69)*

Preserving the bishop. White's next few moves are a wonderful demonstration of resource transference from one side of the board to the other.

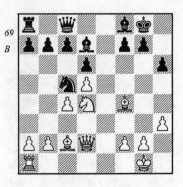

Since Black is short of pieces on the kingside, this is where White concentrates his efforts. Of course he could just as easily swing them from the kingside to the queenside. It would take Black's f8-bishop ages to get to the queenside to help with things there. More relevant here is the amount of time that it takes Black's pieces on the queenside to aid in the black king's defence – assuming it is possible at all.

19 ...   a7-a5

Preventing 20 b2-b4 and so at least securing the knight on c5.

20 ♖a1-e1   ♕c8-d8
21 ♖e1-e3!

White dominates the only open file, but Black is controlling the entry points. Therefore the rook cannot invade the 7th rank, but instead uses the e-file to switch to the kingside.

21 ...   b7-b6
22 ♖e3-g3 *(70)*

All of a sudden White has built up a dangerous attack with the immediate threat being 23 ♝f4xh6.

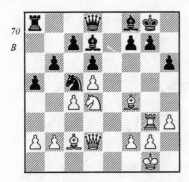

70
B

22 ... &g8-h8
23 ♘d4-f3

The idea behind this move is to vacate the d4-square for either the white queen or the white bishop. Then the g7-pawn would once again be pinned, effectively leaving the h6-pawn *en prise*.

23 ... ♛d8-e7
24 ♛d2-d4 ♛e7-f6

This results in the decisive weakening of Black's kingside pawns. However 24...f7-f6 is no better as after 25 ♘f3-h4, White is attacking with all of his pieces (and Black defending with just two).

25 ♛d4xf6 g7xf6
26 ♘f3-d4 ♖a8-e8
27 ♖g3-e3 ♖e8-b8

White has a winning endgame, with or without the rooks. Hence Black chooses to keep them on in hope of obtaining some counterplay. As it turns out, this simply enables White to terminate the game more quickly.

28 b2-b3 b7-b5
29 c4xb5 ♗d7xb5
30 ♘d4-f5 ♗b5-d7

31 ♘f5xh6 ♖b8-b4
32 ♖e3-g3 ♗f8xh6
33 ♗f4xh6 ♘c5-e4
34 ♗h6-g7+ &h8-h7
35 f2-f3 **1-0**

Q Could having a space advantage ever be a disadvantage?

A Yes, although this is a funny question. Having a space advantage implies having lots of space behind one's own centre pawns (i.e. the further advanced they are, the more space there is). This space can be used for manoeuvring pieces, and this goes for enemy pieces too. In other words, if the opponent could get his pieces around the back of your pawns, then they might wreak havoc. Generally it can be taken for granted that you have these squares covered, but the more bits that are traded off, the more difficult this task becomes. Take a look at the frequently occurring pawn structure (particularly in the French Defence) below:

71

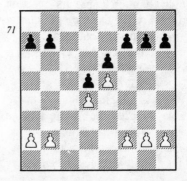

White has a space advantage, but in an endgame this could easily work against him. The centre pawns, which are so often a tower of strength, can often become a liability as White struggles hard to defend his d4-pawn. This is, if you like, the pawn propping up his centre and is much more vulnerable than the equivalent one of Black's on f7. Were Black to get a rook to the c-file then White would have to work hard to guard against a penetration. In contrast if White got a rook to the c-file first, then simply a king on d7 would control all of the entry points. When pawns are far advanced, they are more dangerous and there are sometimes tricks as they are closer to promotion. On the other hand, the further advanced they are, the more difficult they are to defend.

20) The role of the f-pawn

Everyone at some time in their chess playing life has had a disaster due to their king being exposed by the lack of an f-pawn. An amazingly common beginners' reaction to the French Defence provides a good illustrative example:

> 1 e2-e4   e7-e6
> 2 d2-d4   d7-d5
> 3 f2-f3? (72)

This is a logical move in that it seeks to preserve White's pawn centre. However the premature exposure of the white king, combined with the black queen's easy

access to the h4-square, means that the concept is flawed.

> 4 ...   d5xe4
> 5 f3xe4?

Now the pawns look nice, but a lack of piece support (one developed knight would suffice) leaves White in trouble. Interestingly enough, if White played 5 ♘b1-c3 offering a pawn sacrifice, then after 5...e4xf3 (5...♗f8-b4 is better) 6 ♘g1xf3, White has some compensation for the pawn in terms of a lead in development and a couple of useful half-open files. Replace Black's ...e7-e6 with ...♘g8-f6 and in fact we would have the 'Blackmar-Diemer Gambit' (which in all fairness probably isn't very good anyway!).

> 5 ...   ♛d8-h4+

This is pretty grim for White, who must either move his king or lose a rook after 6 g2-g3 ♛h4xe4+.

I find that an interesting statistical curve arrives when observing the use of the f-pawn at different levels of play. For beginners, experiences like the above and the use of bad moves like 2...f7-f6 below, turn them off the idea of moving this pawn completely.

    1 e2-e4   e7-e5
    2 ♘g1-f3   f7-f6? *(73)*

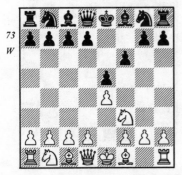

We already know that here Black could defend the e5-pawn adequately with the developing move 2...♘b8-c6, or counter-attack White's e4-pawn with 2...♘g8-f6 (Petroff Defence). The 'Strongpoint Defence', 2...♕d8-e7?! is another wacky invention of the famous chess extrovert, International Master Michael Basman, but an alternative solid opening is the 'Philidor Defence'. This is 2...d6, intending to develop the b8-knight on d7, leaving the c7-pawn free to control the d5-square with a later ...c7-c6.

The text move is weak because when the natural ♗f1-c4 is eventually played, Black will have severe difficulty in castling kingside and, indeed, White can opt for an immediate tactical solution with 3 ♘f3xe5. By leaving the pawn at home (and keeping it defended

when attacked), through lessons learnt, a player will improve. Nevertheless, ignoring the f-pawn is restricting one's options and at higher levels, the f-pawn is once again introduced as an often lethal weapon.

One obvious use that it has is as a pawn break as in the 'Vienna Game' below:

    1 e2-e4   e7-e5
    2 ♘b1-c3

An immediate 2 f2-f4 is, as previously seen, the 'King's Gambit'.

    2 ...   ♘g8-f6
    3 ♗f1-c4

White is delaying ♘g1-f3 as he wants to play f2-f4 first. 3 f2-f4 would be the 'Vienna Gambit'. When this type of opening is met for the first time, there is often a tendency for Black to play too passively. For example, after 3...d7-d6?! 4 ♘g1-f3 ♘b8-c6 5 ♗f1-c4 ♗f8-e7 6 d2-d3 0-0 7 0-0 *(74)*, White has a comfortable space advantage.

White may choose to play f4xe5 later to give himself a half-open f-file. However it is more likely that he will opt to cramp Black's already restricted position with f4-f5. Should he then launch his g-pawn up to g5, Black is forced back even further and then with moves like f5-f6 or g5-g6 available, checkmate is certainly a reality (when the white queen and other pieces enter the attack). Often we are told that one must combat wing play with action in the centre. Although merely playing 3 f2-f4 may not exactly constitute 'wing play', it is perhaps not surprising then that Black's correct response is 3...d7-d5, guaranteeing his pieces a freer game.

3 ...	**♘b8-c6**
4 d2-d3	

White has played cautiously so that when he eventually plays f2-f4, if the pawn is taken, he could recapture immediately with the bishop.

We have just seen how the f-pawn can be used to instigate an attack. For this purpose it definitely is good, but again there is a warning. By moving it, you are conceding squares and sometimes if it gets stuck (i.e. gets blocked or is unable to move further), then it may easily obstruct the path of a bishop.

Other uses of the f-pawn include generally controlling extra centre squares and as we saw earlier (e.g. in the Four Pawns Attack against the Alekhine's Defence), simply supporting the centre.

Q Is the suggested f-pawn move justified in each of the following positions?

a)

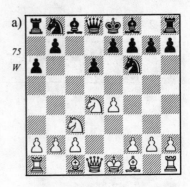

75
W

6 f2-f4

b)

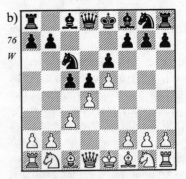

76
W

5 f2-f4

c)

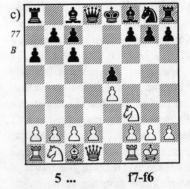

77
B

5 ...   **f7-f6**

d)

78
W

5 f2-f4

e)

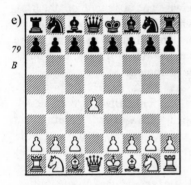

79
B

1 ...   f7-f5

A a) Yes. The reader should by now recognize Black's defence as the Sicilian Najdorf. Whether White castles kingside or queenside, it is a popular recipe for White to launch his kingside pawns in a threatening manner. Black is far more likely to castle kingside. White need not play f2-f4 immediately and instead could, for the time being, refrain from this with 6 ♗f1-e2 for instance. Although other options are available,

this same choice between 6 f2-f4 and 6 ♗f1-e2 is also applicable against the Sicilian Scheveningen (replacing 5...a6 with 5...e6) and the Sicilian Dragon (replacing 5...a6 with ...g6).

b) No. The e5-pawn is not in need of support as it is the d4-pawn which is really coming under fire. The pawn on f4 would limit the scope of the c1-bishop and there is little chance of it making it to f5. In fact after 5 f2-f4? ♕d8-b6 6 ♘g1-f3 ♘g8-h6, White is already in some trouble. He will find it difficult to defend his d4-pawn (necessary in view of ...♘h6-f5) and 7 d4xc5 leaves him with problems on f2 after 7...♗f8xc5.

c) Yes. This is a very satisfactory way of defending the e5-pawn. Note that there will be few problems along the a2-g8 diagonal as White no longer has his light-squared bishop.

d) No. Black can prevent this pawn from advancing with ...♗c8-f5, therefore condemning the c1-bishop to a life of comparative misery. The e3-square would be weakened and in contrast to e4, e5 would not be an outpost.

e) Yes, but it wouldn't suit everyone. The opening is the 'Dutch Defence' and in controlling a centre square, there is a clear similarity with the Sicilian Defence. The big difference is that it's on the kingside, making things a little more risky. 1...f7-f5 has an aggressive reputation and it appears that White has just two methods of dealing with it. Firstly he can fight fire with fire with 2 e2-e4 (the Staunton Gambit) or the aggressive alternatives 2 ♘b1-c3 and 2 ♗c1-g5. Dwelling on the latter for a moment, the following game demonstrates how, very occasionally, opening rules can be blatantly disregarded, with reasonable justification:

Ward-G.Wall
National Chess League 1994

1 d2-d4   f7-f5
2 ♗c1-g5

The aim of this move (a bishop before a knight) is to disrupt Black's kingside development, so for example 2...♘g8-f6 can be met by 3 ♗g5xf6 e7xf6 4 e2-e3 and White has a positional edge. Note that the exposure of Black's king is highlighted if he tries to trap the bishop with 2...h7-h6 3 ♗g5-h4 g7-g5 4 e2-e3! g5xh4?? 5 ♕d1-h5 mate.

2 ...   c7-c5

Black attacks White's centre and facilitates a future ...♕d8-b6 to exploit the lack of protection for the b2-pawn.

3 d4xc5   ♘b8-a6

Knights on the rim are dim, but this one threatens to recapture the pawn, from where it has a big influence on the centre.

4 e2-e4   f5xe4 *(80)*

Already an incredible position. My opponent now has three centre pawns and a knight on the rim, whilst I have developed a solitary bishop and given away my centre pawns – all in the name of quick development.

5 ♗f1xa6?!

Removing Black's only developed piece was very tempting, but I should have resisted it in favour of 5 ♘b1-c3!. Then after 5...♘a6xc5 6 ♗g5-e3, 6...♘c5-e6 7 ♘c3xe4 leaves White with a clear advantage and 6...b7-b6 7 ♗e3xc5 b6xc5 *(81)* allows White a delightful winning theme:

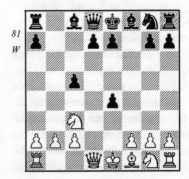

8 ♕d1-h5+ g7-g6 9 ♕h5-d5 ♖a8-b8 10 ♕d5-e5 or 8 ♕d1-d5 ♖a8-b8 9 ♕d5-h5+ g7-g6 10 ♕h5-e5, both methods bagging at least a piece.

5 ...	b7xa6
6 ♘b1-c3	♗c8-b7
7 ♕d1-d4	♘g8-f6
8 0-0-0	♕d8-c7
9 ♗g5xf6	g7xf6

Black shortly catches up on development and, besides, always has compensation because of his bishop pair.

10 ♘c3-d5	♕c7-c6
11 ♕d4xe4	0-0-0
12 ♕e4-f4	e7-e6
13 ♘d5-e3	♗f8xc5
14 ♘g1-f3	♖h8-f8?
15 ♖d1-d3	d7-d5
16 ♘f3-d4	♗c5xd4
17 ♕e4xd4	♔c8-b8?
18 f2-f4	♖d8-c8
19 f4-f5	e6xf5

Things have gone horribly wrong for Black, who now has a poor bishop and six isolated pawns.

20 ♖h1-f1	♖f8-e8
21 ♖d3-c3	♕c6-d6
22 ♖c3xc8+	♔b8xc8
23 ♘e3xf5	♕d6xh2
24 ♕d4xf6	♔c8-b8
25 ♘f5-d6	1-0

The queen and knight are known as the most deadly attacking force. Indeed with his queen out of play, Black is unable to defend his rook and his king. The reader should not attach too much significance to this game. This crazy sort of play is very rarely acceptable.

Anyway, the above was an example of fighting fire with fire, but in fact the most popular reply to 1...f7-f5 at top flight is 2 g2-g3. If the f8-bishop is destined for d6 (say in a 'Stonewall' structure with pawns on c6, d5, e6 and f5), then this a good way of negating Black's aggression. Even if Black fianchettoes his dark-squared bishop (known as the 'Leningrad Dutch'), then White's light-squared bishop will bear down on Black's queenside and he might later follow up c2-c4 with further queenside expansion.

21) Knights and Bishops

It is about time that I said a few words on the key issue of which are better, bishops or knights. When asked this question the standard answer that is given is that it 'depends on the position'. Of course this is very true, the simple explanation being that the long-range power of the bishop gives it the advantage over a knight in an endgame (with pawns on both sides). Knights, we are told, prefer closed positions, where in contrast to bishops, they can take their time to hop to any available good squares.

It is definitely the case that due to their 'jazzy' forking ability, beginners have a fondness for knights. All strong players will admit that in time trouble, dealing with knights can be a nightmare (excuse the pun), but other than this, with all other things equal, bishops are considered better than knights. Of course there are always plenty of other factors at any time to be taken into consideration.

Bishops are superior in open positions, where their diagonals are not obstructed, but as far as knights go, the more fixed pawns the better (if there must be pawns, a bishop prefers them flexible, so as not to get permanently rendered 'bad').

The following classic game puts the knight in a very good light:

Fischer-Olicio Gadia
Mar del Plata 1960

1	e2-e4	c7-c5
2	♘g1-f3	d7-d6
3	d2-d4	c5xd4
4	♘f3xd4	♘g8-f6
5	♘b1-c3	a7-a6
6	♗f1-c4	

Bobby Fischer was an expert in the Sicilian Najdorf himself, but he pioneered this 'Sozin-Najdorf' variation when he came up against his own favourite defence. More recently its popularity has soared thanks to its resurrection by Nigel Short in his PCA World Championship clash with Garry Kasparov.

6	...	e7-e6
7	♗c4-b3	b7-b5
8	0-0	♗c8-b7
9	f2-f4	♘b8-c6

10	♘d4xc6	♗b7xc6
11	f4-f5	e7-e5
12	♕d1-d3	♗f8-e7

Up until now the game has been quite tactical, with Fischer happy to sacrifice a pawn for an attack. However, the game now becomes very positional, with White demonstrating exquisitely how to occupy and then utilize the outpost on d5.

13 ♗g5! *(82)*

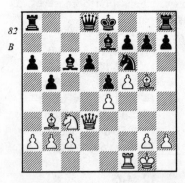

White sets about liquidating the black pieces which look over the outpost. Hence the only minor piece that White is not interested in is the e7-bishop.

13	...	♕d8-b6+
14	♔g1-h1	0-0
15	♗g5xf6	♗e7xf6
16	♗b3-d5!	

Stage two of the master plan. After 16 ♘c3-d5 ♗c6xd5 17 ♗b3xd5, the bishop is well placed. Nevertheless, it is really a knight that White would prefer on this outpost. Hence the text move.

16	...	♖a8-c8

17	&d5xc6	&c8xc6
18	&a1-d1	&f8-c8
19	&c3-d5	&b6-d8 *(83)*

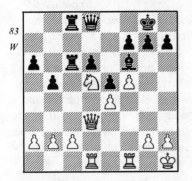

83
W

White has finally achieved his aim, and is he going to engage in a fair trade for Black's bishop? No chance! Instead after removing any Black counterplay (i.e. blocking the c-file), he seeks to find some action for his comparatively redundant pieces (the rooks).

20	c2-c3	&f6-e7
21	&d1-a1	f7-f6
22	a2-a4	

White is intending to get his rooks onto the 7th rank via the a-file. As it transpires, he doesn't need to follow through with this devastating process, as Black, under severe pressure, immediately blunders.

22	...	&c8-b8
23	&d5xe7+	1-0

Finally White concedes his excellent knight for Black's 'bad' bishop. This is only because after 23...&d8xe7, 24 &d3-d5+ wins a rook.

An excellent game, but by no means a typical example. Often with plenty of pieces on the board, even a supposedly bad bishop can outshine a knight. Knights generally like to have at least one pawn to look after them, and without such support, in open positions they can be extremely vulnerable. The point is that a bishop can rest at one end of the board and yet influence the other end, whereas in comparison, a knight must actually *be* there to be in on the action.

Another vital point to note is that while one often hears others talking about having the advantage of a bishop for a knight, this advantage may in fact lie in having the bishop pair. Having the power of the two bishops implies that even if one of them is bad, then often the 'goodness' of the other over-compensates. Particularly in open positions where both light-squares and dark-squares are controlled, the edge of having two bishops against a bishop and a knight (or two knights), can often prove decisive. At the very least they hold the latent threat of being absolutely wicked in endgames.

For the reasons described so far, my advice is that one should not casually concede bishops for knights. Indeed, bishops often pin knights, but with the exception of totally ruining the enemy pawn structure, actually have no intention of giving themselves up for the pinned knight. Likewise when given the choice of winning either a bishop or a knight, or having to give up one of the two, again more often than not the bishop will get the nod. Take for example the following:

1 e2-e4   e7-e5
2 ♘g1-f3   ♘b8-c6
3 ♗f1-c4   ♘g8-f6

The 'Two Knights Defence', the main alternative being 3...♗f8-c5.

4 ♘b1-c3?! *(84)*

84
B

A natural-looking move, but in fact White pays the price for not seeking a pawn break (he should probably be looking to play c2-c3 to support a later d3-d4). Better are 4 d2-d3, 4 d2-d4 and 4 ♘f3-g5 (all covered in Chapter 4).

4 ...   ♘f6xe4!

A fine though simple tactical concept, which leaves Black at least equal.

5 ♘c3xe4

There is a temptation for White to believe that if he must concede

a minor piece then he can at least draw the black king out with 5 ♗c4xf7+?!. However after 5...♔e8xf7 6 ♘c3xe4 d7-d5 7 ♘e4-g5+ ♔f7-g8, a closer inspection shows that it is White who is in trouble. OK, Black can't castle, but he can manoeuvre his king to h7. He has a bishop for a knight, two excellent centre pawns and a handy half-open f-file. All White has to show for a couple of useless checks are two very awkwardly placed offside knights.

5 ...   d7-d5
6 ♕d1-e2?

Giving Black the chance to take the better minor piece. 6 ♗c4-d3 is probably correct, but the other bishop-preserving move 6 ♗c4-b5?! d5xe4 7 ♘f3xe5 fails to the startling queen intervention, 7...♕d8-g5!, hitting the g2-pawn, the e5-knight and through it the bishop on b5. Many would resign themselves to an inferior position with 6 ♗c4xd5 ♕d8xd5. Then after 7 ♘e4-c3 ♕d5-d8, White has a slight lead in development, but Black has a good centre pawn and the advantage of having the two bishops.

6 ...   d5xc4!
7 ♕e2xc4

Now White's queen is out as well, giving Black the chance to develop while attacking it.

7 ...   ♗c8-e6
8 ♕c4-e2   ♗f8-e7
9 d2-d3   0-0

10 ♗c1-e3   f7-f5
11 ♘e4-c5 *(85)*

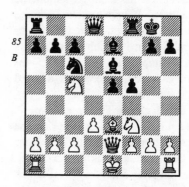

85
B

The white knight is on a very good square and after 11...♗e7xc5 12 ♗e3xc5 ♖f8-e8, Black retains a small plus. Nevertheless he can maximize his advantage by preserving his bishops. Indeed even the 'undeveloping' 11...♗e6-c8 is worthy of a lot of consideration. The point is that Black is having to keep his patience and handle the knight, but with the intention of kicking it away with 12...b7-b6. Then the knight would be pushed back to the rather ineffective b3-square and Black's light-squared bishop could resurface safely again on e6 or perhaps b7. A golden rule then seems to be to hold back on giving up a bishop for a knight for as long as is possible (as you might not have to do so at all).

Q Which of the suggested moves are preferable in the following positions?

a)

86
W

3 ♗g5xf6 or 3 ♘g1-f3

b)

87
W

5 ♗g5xf6 or 5 ♗g5-h4

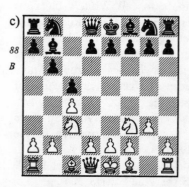

c)

88
B

4...♘g8-f6 or 4...♗b7xf3

d)
89
W

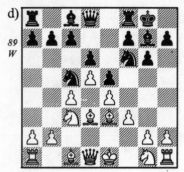

9 ♗e3xc5, 9 ♘g1-e2 or 9 ♗d3-c2

A a) Either. The 'Trompowsky' opening is 1 d2-d4 ♘g8-f6 2 ♗c1-g5. White justifies this early bishop move by claiming that he is threatening 3 ♗g5xf6. This weakens Black's pawn structure, and such a concession (of bishop for knight) is followed by a plan of keeping the position relatively closed. Some fear this pawn doubling and continue with 2...♘f6-e4 (moving one piece twice, but gaining a tempo on the g5-bishop), but others may choose to call White's bluff (as here) with 2...d7-d5. Recently the leading pioneer of this sharp opening, Grandmaster Julian Hodgson, said that he has a problem now because he has grown quite fond of positions where he has the two bishops! Fortunately for him there is a suitable alternative in the 'Torre Attack', usually arrived at by 1 d2-d4 ♘g8-f6 2 ♘g1-f3 d7-d5 (or 2...e7-e6) 3 ♗c1-g5, i.e. from diagram (a) a direct transposition is available with 3 ♘g1-f3. The c2-c4 (Queen's Gambit) option should not be ruled out, but the super-solid development scheme in the Torre (and indeed the 'London System' which merely puts the bishop on f4 instead of g5) involves c2-c3, e2-e3, ♗f1-d3, 0-0 and ♘b1-d2.

b) 5 ♗g5-h4. This is an example of a pin, where unless Black can be forced to play ...g7xf6, White has little intention of taking the knight. Indeed after 5 ♗g5xf6?!, if Black returns the favour immediately with 5...♗b4xc3+ 6 b2xc3 ♕d8xf6, and continues by transfering his pawns to dark squares (i.e. ...d7-d6 and ...e6-e5 freeing his remaining bishop), then he already stands better.

c) 4...♗b7xf3. 4...♘g8-f6 is satisfactory, but here Black has a rare chance to concede a fianchettoed bishop favourably. After 4...♗b7xf3! 5 e2xf3, the compensation Black has for this trade is in the form of a beautiful outpost on d4. He should seek to occupy this square with a knight and if necessary control it further with a kingside fianchetto.

d) 9 ♗d3-c2. Clearly bad and indeed a common mistake is 9 ♗e3xc5. This is White's good bishop and although the King's Indian bishop on g7 doesn't look great, these bishops have a mysterious way of finding play and if this does, then White will need his dark-squared bishop to cover any holes. Besides, the e3-bishop, which eyes up both the kingside and the queenside, is an excellent piece. The main difficulty in this position is understanding why White should want to remove his bad bishop from the evil clutches of the well placed knight on c5. The simple answer is that when White forces this knight away with b2-b4 (aiming for a later c4-c5) his bishop can get around the back (probably at least being able to swap itself for Black's good bishop) whilst the knight will get in the way of all Black's other cramped pieces and probably end up a liability. OK, so it's not quite that straightforward, as Black will undoubtedly play 9...a7-a5. Nevertheless White can aim to play b2-b4, if necessary with b2-b3, a2-a3 and perhaps even ♖a1-b1 first. Meanwhile, should Black go for the traditional ...f7-f5 pawn break, White will find his bishop performing a function along the b1-h7 diagonal. The other basic logic of course is that White has a space advantage and so should try to avoid exchanges.

22) The stereotyped set-up

Having got this far, the reader should now be aware of the fact that there is no ideal allocation of pieces. There is not a perfect square that has a given piece's name on it! Only too often you

hear novices (particularly juniors) implying that something like the following is the 'best set-up':

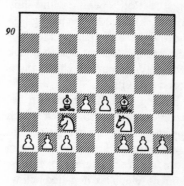

Of course there are variations on this theme, with the bishops one square further out or perhaps the knights tucked in on e2 and d2. The truth of course is that no such perfect arrangements exist. Beginners textbooks often suggest various piece placements, but in reality, where you put your pieces depends upon where your opponent's pieces are (or at least where you anticipate they will be).

In my view, the closest one can get to constantly adopting the same piece formation is with the King's Indian Defence and the Pirc Defence. These defences (the former a standard queen's pawn defence and the latter a standard king's pawn defence) both involve a kingside fianchetto by Black. Indeed many good players have both these openings in their repertoire. This is of course very acceptable and, bearing in mind the similarity of plans, probably quite sensible. However it then becomes a little sad if these same players adopt, say, the 'Réti' opening with White (1 ♘g1-f3 intending to play g2-g3 shortly) as their games then become rather tedious due to a lack of variety. Remember chess is supposed to be fun!

Having said this, there is a defensive structure for Black which appears to crop up in a lot of high level games. This set-up occurs from several different openings, three of which are depicted below:

1 c2-c4   c7-c5

White has played the English Opening and for obvious reasons this variation is known as the 'Symmetrical English'.

2 ♘g1-f3   ♘g8-f6
3 g2-g3   b7-b6
4 ♗f1-g2   ♗c8-b7
5 0-0   e7-e6

It is not so often that one fianchettoes both bishops. The argument against such a procedure is that bishops like to work together, thus radiating their dual power, rather than engaging in a crossfire. However, every now and then it is reasonable to have one bishop exerting pressure on the enemy queenside, with the other firing upon the kingside. Here for example 5...g7-g6 is very playable and is known as the 'Double Fianchetto' variation.

6 ♘b1-c3   ♗f8-e7
7 d2-d4   c5xd4

8 ♕d1xd4

Whilst 8 ♘f3xd4 is also fine, the text is more popular because it keeps more pieces on the board. There is a subtle point here which is that although Black can develop his b8-knight to c6 now, gaining a tempo on the white queen, frequently he prefers to place it on d7. Both the black queen and a white rook are destined for the c-file. With a knight on c6, Black would then be vulnerable to a ♘c3-d5 tactic.

8 ...   d7-d6
9 ♖f1-d1   0-0
10 b2-b3   ♘b8-d7
11 ♗c1-b2   a7-a6 *(91)*

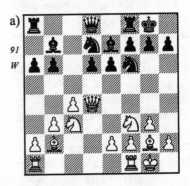

a)

91
W

1 e2-e4   c7-c5
2 ♘g1-f3   e7-e6
3 d2-d4   c5xd4
4 ♘f3xd4   ♘b8-c6

Initiating the 'Taimanov' variation of the Sicilian.

5 ♘d4-b5

White breaks a rule in order to seal in Black's dark-squared bishop. If Black has to concede his f8-bishop for this knight (White has 6 ♘b5-d6+ in mind), then his dark squares will be terribly weakened. 5 ♘b1-c3 is also sensible, but if White tried to establish a bind with 5 c2-c4, then the importance of the text manoeuvre is highlighted as Black would be fine after 5...♘g8-f6 6 ♘b1-c3 ♗f8-b4.

5 ...   d7-d6

The problem with 5...d7-d5 is not so much that it results in an isolated pawn after 6 e4xd5 e6xd5, but that this pawn can be captured: 7 ♕d1xd5! ♕d8xd5 8 ♘b5-c7+.

6 c2-c4   ♘g8-f6
7 ♘b1-c3   a7-a6
8 ♘b5-a3

This knight is now a little offside, but the important thing for White is that, for the time being at least, he is preventing Black's two key pawn breaks: ...b7-b5 and ...d7-d5.

8 ...   b7-b6
9 ♗f1-e2

This is definitely a more accurate move than 9 ♗f1-d3, as the bishop is more vulnerable to black knights there.

9 ...   ♗c8-b7
10 0-0

The immediate 10 f2-f4 is probably more aggressive allowing for 11 ♗e2-f3, protecting the e-pawn without blocking the f-pawn.

10 ...   ♘c6-b8
11 f2-f3   ♘b8-d7
12 ♗c1-e3   ♗f8-e7 *(92)*

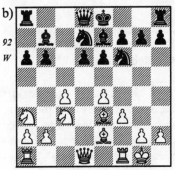

1 d2-d4   ♘g8-f6
2 ♘g1-f3   e7-e6
3 e2-e3

Whether White intends a later b2-b3 or c2-c3, this rather unadventurous opening is called the 'Colle System'.

3 ...   c7-c5
4 ♗f1-d3   c5xd4
5 e3xd4   b7-b6
6 0-0   ♗c8-b7
7 b2-b3

7 c2-c3 and 7 c2-c4 are both possible, whilst 7 ♗c1-g5 transposes to the 'Torre Attack'.

7 ...   ♗f8-e7
8 ♗c1-b2   0-0
9 c2-c4   d7-d6
10 ♘b1-d2   ♘b8-d7 *(93)*

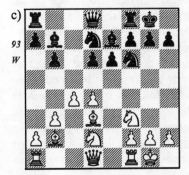

Q Assuming that there was no individual inventor of this piece and pawn formation, how might you name it?

A Not exactly the world's most relevant question, and I obviously don't know what name you selected, but it is actually called the 'Hedgehog'. It is not immediately clear why it is so labelled, except that it is *not* named after a Mr Hedgehog! The reason, we are told, is that White must be careful how he handles the opening, for if he tries too hard to crush Black, then he might just wind up impaled on Black's prickly spikes. Well, something like that anyway! Clearly Black's piece arrangement in diagrams (a), (b), and (c) is practically identical. Often the main plan involves waiting for White to commit himself and then going on the counter-attack. Meanwhile having castled, Black can (in (a) and (b) anyway) play moves like ...♛d8-c7, ...♜f8-e8, ...♜a8-d8(or c8). In all cases the e7-bishop can drop back to f8, from where it is often fianchettoed. Occasionally one sees Black having prickly spikes (i.e. pawns) on a6, b6, d6, e6, g6, and sometimes even h6. In the illustrated positions, Black's main weakness is the d6-pawn. However White seems to have difficulty in attacking it, particularly with minor pieces, and Black always seems to

be able to muster adequate defences. Black is very solid in (c), and in (a) and (b) (true Hedgehogs due to the half-open d-file), in practice it seems that if Black ever gets in the freeing ...b6-b5 or ...d6-d5, then more often than not it is White who is in trouble.

23) The exposed king and the early queen trade

In section 7 the reader was given some hardly precise advice about being sure to castle around about the early stages of the game, with exceptions. Very enlightening! Then in section 20, we saw how the f-pawn can be a very valuable commodity, even though moving it often means less protection for one's own king. I would be the first to admit that a lot of this book's sections have included some rather vague details and I'm afraid the same can be said about the definition of an 'exposed king'. In general an exposed king is one which is fairly open. It might, for example, have no pawns around it and/or no local pieces to help in its defence. This does not necessarily mean it is a bad thing; as with most things, it depends on the position. If a king is unlikely to be in any danger, then why should it have pieces around it that could be far better employed elsewhere? Ultimately everything is down to judgement, but in order to make such conscious decisions, one must be aware of such possibilities in the first place.

Take a very simple example:

1 e2-e4	e7-e6
2 d2-d4	d7-d5
3 e4xd5	

White opts to play the 'Exchange Variation' against the French Defence.

| 3 ... | e6xd5 *(94)* |

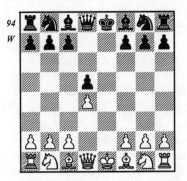

Here the black king is exposed along the a4-e8 diagonal and similarly the white king along the a5-e1 diagonal. However, these are not a problem, whereas the presence of an open e-file is. If one side now managed to conjure up a rook here (say by the white king and rook trading places) then a check would have to be blocked by a piece. This would then be setting up a self-pin. OK, so checkmate would still be far off, but nonetheless with pieces pinned to the king, things are often very awkward and at best one's own plans are put on ice for quite a while.

It would therefore be safe to assume that, be it kingside or queenside, both sides would be eager to castle. With a similar logic, now 4 ♕d1-e2+? would be a pathetic move. Then after 4...♗f8-e7 Black is nearer to castling and with ...♘g8-f6, ...0-0, and ...♖f8-e8 coming next, White could easily find himself very embarrassed.

Slightly outside the scope of this book is the advice that kings are very useful in the endgame. If the queens get swapped off then often correct logic is that there is no need to castle as the king will only need to re-emerge shortly to make an impact on the game. This doesn't *always* hold, since 'having the queens off' isn't necessarily the only factor determining whether a position is in its opening, middlegame or endgame stage. While it is certainly useful, the queen is by no means obligatory to give checkmate. The rooks and the minor pieces are quite capable of inflicting damage.

The point I am trying to make is that if it involves trading queens, one should not base a whole plan around preventing an opponent from castling. A good example of this is in the 'Old Indian Defence'.

1 d2-d4	♘g8-f6
2 c2-c4	d7-d6
3 ♘b1-c3	e7-e5
4 d4xe5	

Not exactly a bad move, but as this basically swaps his d4-pawn for the black d6-pawn, 4 ♘g1-f3 (intending 5 e2-e4 or 5 g2-g3) would probably be more testing.

4	...	d6xe5
5	♕d1xd8+	♚e8xd8
6	♗c1-g5	c7-c6
7	0-0-0+	♚d8-c7 *(95)*

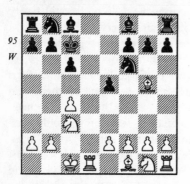

95
W

The black king has found itself a comfortable home which is not far from the centre for when the endgame comes in earnest. If White were now to play 8 e2-e4?! then Black would have an outpost on d4, but White no equivalent one on d5 (note the c6-pawn is very important). Were Black to continue from here with the sensible 8 ♘g1-f3 then Black should reply with 8...♘b8-d7.

Q Above after 8 ♘g1-f3 ♘f6-d7?, how could White win a pawn?

A With 9 ♘f3xe5 as 9...♘d7xe5?? would allow 10 ♗g5-d8 mate. I said the king

was comfortable, but I didn't say Black didn't have to be careful!

24) 'Blocking up' and 'Maintaining the tension'

I have already talked a lot about closed positions and open positions. We know that knights prefer things blocked, provided that there is room for them to manoeuvre, whereas we know that bishops aren't so keen on fixed pawns and enjoy more flexibility in the structure. We also understand that kings are generally safe in the centre with pawn blockages in front of them (although castling may be required to free a rook). These are just some of the factors that I feel aren't given adequate consideration by many players when deciding on whether to advance a pawn, thus effectively sealing off a part of the board. I am of course referring to situations in which pawns are in direct conflict and whilst pushing on or exchanging appear the easy options, often the alternative of 'maintaining the tension' (i.e. not committing the pawn) is the superior one. With both sides often jockeying for position in the centre, such situations are indeed very common (we have just seen one in the Old Indian Defence). Remember the reader himself should now be looking either to make that initial pawn break or perhaps strike out in the centre.

Below we see for the first time the slightly unusual 'Nimzowitsch Defence':

1 e2-e4   ♞b8-c6
2 d2-d4   d7-d6

One line is for Black to strike out immediately with 2...d7-d5. Then White would have the familiar choice: advance (3 e4-e5), exchange (3 e4xd5), or maintain the tension with 3 ♞b1-c3.

3 ♞g1-f3   e7-e5?! *(96)*

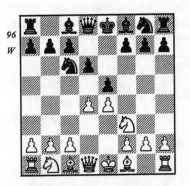

96
W

This is not the main intention of this opening, with Black usually playing either 3...♞g8-f6 or 3...♝c8-g4.

Q What are White's options in this position?

A The instinctive reaction here might be to play the space-gaining 4 d4-d5 and then after 4...♞c6-e7, follow up with 5 c2-c4. With Black aiming for the ...f7-f5 pawn break and possibly solving the problem of what to do with his f8-bishop with a kingside

fianchetto, it is not unlikely that play will take on characteristics of the King's Indian Defence.

After 4 d4xe5 ♞c6xe5, White stands a little better but for reasons already stated would have no real advantage in the endgame arrived at by 5 ♞f3xe5 d6xe5 6 ♛d1xd8+ ♚e8xd8.

Possibly the best idea for White would be to keep the tension in the centre. He might choose to exert further pressure on Black's e5-pawn with 4 ♝f1-b5. Also he could add more support to his d4-pawn with 4 c2-c3 or just develop with 4 ♝f1-c4.

25) Traps

I am afraid the reader will be disappointed now if he expected this section to include a long list of opening traps. For some unknown reason we all enjoy our opponents falling for tricks early on, often leading to a quick win. I have had several opponents caught by the same pitfall and I believe it is sad that some sadistic streak means that I often derive as much satisfaction from these short victories as from the hard-fought wins.

My point is that bearing in mind everything else in this book, there is no justification for going out of one's way in order to set an opening trap (later on, maybe, if you are losing!). If your opponent is going to be dumb enough to fall for a cheap trick, then it is safe to assume that you would have beaten him during the course of a normally played game. On the other hand, if you compromise your position and your opponent is blessed with a higher IQ than expected, then you have given yourself a disadvantage before the real battle begins. Take the following:

1 e2-e4   e7-e5
2 ♘g1-f3   ♘b8-c6
3 ♗f1-c4   ♘c6-d4 *(97)*

Nicknamed the 'Oh my God' trap, because in order to achieve full effect, this crafty move is supposed to be accompanied by a highly illegal but very audible 'Oh my God!', thus (theoretically) removing any doubts that one really has just blundered. Assuming that one's opponent isn't the suspicious type, then the best scenario is 4 ♘f3xe5? (falling hook, line and sinker) 4...♕d8-g5 5 ♘e5xf7 ♕g5xg2 6 ♖h1-f1 ♕g2xe4+ 7 ♗c4-e2 ♘d4-f3 mate. However, assuming that your opponent wasn't born yesterday, then any

sensible move (like 4 c2-c3, 4 0-0 or 4 ♘f3xd4) will be sufficient to punish your moving the same piece twice, by leaving White with a very comfortable edge. The most common reason for walking into traps is through inadequate development. If you are sticking to the opening rules and your opponent isn't, then he might find himself falling for a trap that you didn't even go out of your way to set. A pretty example shows Black punished for playing an unnecessary pawn move and developing a bishop before a knight:

1 e2-e4   e7-e5
2 ♘g1-f3   d7-d6
3 ♗f1-c4   h7-h6?
4 ♘b1-c3   ♗c8-g4? *(98)*

5 ♘f3xe5!   ♗g4xd1

Naïve to the end. 5...d6xe5, losing a pawn and a bishop for a knight is, if you like, 'better' – although due to Black's lack of development, possibly the text is less painful!

6 ♗c4xf7+   ♔e8-e7
7 ♘c3-d5 mate

In spite of the above, every now and again an opening appears in which traps are set with both sides playing justified moves. One good example of this is the 'Caro-Kann Defence', the following variation proving to be a real minefield:

1 e2-e4   c7-c6
2 d2-d4   d7-d5

In a similar fashion to the French Defence, Black stakes his claim in the centre. In fact White's choice of responses is identical to that in the French, with the exception that here 3 f2-f3 (the 'Fantasy' variation) is playable. A fundamental difference between the two defences can be seen after 3 e4-e5 (the 'Advance' variation in both openings). In the Caro-Kann the c8-bishop is not blocked and so he can play 3...♗c8-f5 (to get his bishop outside the pawn chain) before ...e7-e6. Nevertheless sooner or later in both openings Black is going to want to challenge White's centre with his c-pawn. In the French, he doesn't lose a tempo as he will be advancing this pawn (...c7-c5) for the first time.

3 ♘b1-c3   d5xe4
4 ♘c3xe4   ♘b8-d7

Preparing ...♘g8-f6 when an exchange would not involve his pawns being doubled. Nevertheless 4...♘g8-f6 is a playable variation, as is 4...♗c8-f5.

5 ♘e4-g5 *(99)*

Moving this knight three times in a row appears unbelievable, but White has the plan of trying to make Black play ...e7-e6 before getting his c8-bishop out. The logic is that then Black would be more cramped. Trap number one is that if Black now innocently continues with 5...h7-h6?, then White has 6 ♘g5-e6!. Obviously 6...f7xe6 then allows 7 ♕d1-h5+ mating, but another pitfall is 6...♕d8-a5+ 7 ♗c1-d2 ♕a5-b6 8 ♗f1-d3 f7xe6? (but otherwise White could take the bishop on f8 at any time and have a clear advantage) 9 ♕d1-h5+ ♔e8-d8 10 ♗d2-a5, winning the black queen.

5 ...   ♘g8-f6
6 ♗f1-c4   e7-e6
7 ♕d1-e2 *(100)*

Black's position looks solid enough, but White, whose last move looks as though he might simply be preparing to castle queenside, has another wicked threat up his sleeve. If, for example 7...h7-h6?, then 8 ♘g5xf7! ♔e8xf7 9 ♕e2xe6+ ♔f7-g6 10

♗c4-d3+ ♔g6-h5 11 ♕e6-h3
mate.

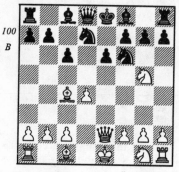

100
B

| 8 ... | ♞d7-b6 |
| 9 ♗c4-d3 | |

The last two tricks in this line also apply to the reasonable alternative 9 ♗c4-b3.

| 9 ... | h7-h6 |

Carefully avoiding 9...♕d8xd4?
10 ♞g1-f3 ♕d4-d8 11 ♞f3-e5! when Black is in deep trouble on f7.

10 ♞g5-f3	c6-c5
11 d4xc5	♗f8xc5
12 ♞f3-e5	♕d8-c7 (101)

101
W

White has had his fun and has emerged with a slight advantage.

Nevertheless now it is he who must tread carefully.

Q What trick is Black now threatening?

A Should White now play an innocuous move like 13 c2-c3? (13 ♞g1-f3 is best), then Black has 13...♗c5xf2+! as Black regains his piece after 14 ♕e2xf2 ♕c7xe5+ or 14 ♔e1xf2 ♕c7xe5! 15 ♕e2xe5 ♞f6-g4+.

26) Gambits

I thought that I had better finish off this chapter with the popular obsession of many club players. Again, for some unknown reason, the concept of giving up a pawn or two in the opening appeals to a large number of chess enthusiasts as a way of making life more exciting. In fact at top levels, genuine gambits are rarely seen. During the course of a game, a player could sacrifice material at any stage, but an opening gambit involves the immediate offering of pawns (and occasionally pieces), usually in order to gain a quick lead in development. There is a definite connection between this section and the last as we already know that one is more likely to walk into a trap when under-developed. Let us see a successful gambit in operation:

| 1 d2-d4 | d7-d5 |
| 2 c2-c4 | e7-e5 (102) |

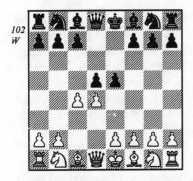

The 'Albin Counter-Gambit'. Interestingly enough my own two quickest wins are playing this gambit and playing White against this gambit!

   3 d4xe5   d5-d4
   4 e2-e3?

White foresees problems with his f1-bishop. He wants to develop it, so he can castle, but should probably do so by engaging in a kingside fianchetto (e.g. 4 ♘g1-f3 ♘b8-c6 5 g2-g3).

   4 ...   ♝f8-b4+
   5 ♗c1-d2   d4xe3
   6 ♗d2xb4

The ugly 6 f2xe3 is objectively better, but Black is on top after 6...♛d8-h4+ 7 g2-g3 ♛h4-e4 (threatening 8...♛e4xh1, 8...♛e4xe5 and 8...♛e4xe3+).

   6 ...   e3xf2+
   7 ♚e1-e2 *(103)*
   7 ...   f2xg1=♘+!

A beautiful finesse leaving White a piece down as 8 ♚e2-e1 is forced due to 8 ♖h1xg1? ♗c8-g4+ winning the white queen. Although a big trap was involved

here, this is perhaps not a good example as it was Black's d-pawn (to e-pawn to f-pawn!) that seemed to win him the day rather than speedy development and active piece play.

The 'Danish Gambit' shows more typical attributes:

   1 e2-e4   e7-e5
   2 d2-d4   e5xd4
   3 c2-c3

We saw much earlier why 3 ♛d1xd4 doesn't really hit the mark. Instead here White demonstrates his eagerness to off-load pawns at a rapid rate.

   3 ...   d4xc3
   4 ♗f1-c4   c3xb2
   5 ♗c1xb2 *(104)*

White has compensation for his two pawn deficit in the form of two already developed raking bishops. With no development whatsoever, it is not difficult to see how any false steps could be disastrous for Black, who has his f7-pawn under close scrutiny.

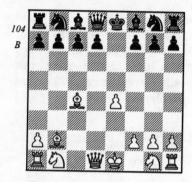

104
B

A common, and sometimes un-necessary, reaction to gambits is to return the material gained. Here for instance Black could start with 5...d7-d5 when after 6 ♗c4xd5 ♘g8-f6 he gains a tempo on the white bishop. Evidently it's not as simple as that, with the amusing road to equality being 7 ♗d5xf7+ ♚e8xf7 8 ♕d1xd8 ♗f8-b4+ 9 ♕d8-d2.

I have already stated that in general gambits do not have a good reputation. The simple logic is that a strong player can accept the offering(s), play carefully, consolidate his position, neutralize the gambiteer's activity and then swap off and win the endgame!

Alternatively, it is very common on the tournament scene to see players not accepting an offered gambit. In declining it (which is often very reasonable) they intend to 'spoil the party'. Perhaps this is not in the spirit of things, but as accepting gambits often implies a certain amount of impending de-fending, obviously not everyone is

game. One should be warned though that although statements like 'I prefer attacking to defend-ing' are quite common, it is better that one becomes well versed in both these styles of play (though not start a game with the intention of either!).

We have already come across the King's Gambit. This aggres-sive opening, illustrated below, is very popular amongst 'hackers' (a slang term referring to those cut-throat players who don't like beat-ing about the bush and like to get straight down to the business of delivering checkmate):

1 e2-e4   e7-e5
2 f2-f4 *(105)*

105
B

Black has three possibilities here. He can:

a) Accept the gambit and then, in slightly risky fashion, try to hold on to the gambit pawn, e.g. 2...e5xf4 3 ♘g1-f3 (guarding against the black queen check on h4, although it must be said that more crazy lines even allow this, such as the Mason Gambit, 3 ♘b1-

c3 ♕d8-h4+ 4 ♔e2) 3...d7-d6 4 d2-d4 g7-g5 5 ♗f1-c4, when White has a nice lead in development for his sacrificed pawn.

b) Decline the gambit with, say, 2...♗f8-c5. Black intends the follow-up of ...d7-d6 and ...♘b8-c6 and White, unlike in the mirror image defence on the queenside (see section 10), is unable to play 3 f4xe5 because of 3...♕d8-h4+.

c) Hit back at White with a counter-gambit. This is not always possible, but here after 2...d7-d5 (the Falkbeer Counter-Gambit), 3 e4xd5 e5-e4, it is White who is a pawn up!

Next up is the 'Smith-Morra Gambit' against the Sicilian Defence:

> **1 e2-e4   c7-c5**
> **2 d2-d4   c5xd4**
> **3 c2-c3** *(106)*

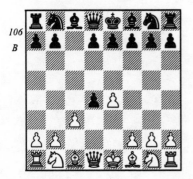

106
B

This is also quite popular at club level. The idea is that after 3...d4xc3 4 ♘b1xc3, White technically has a lead in development (a pawn on e4 and a knight on c3 compared to nothing out for Black) with further swift, free-flowing piece deployments to follow.

Q If so desired, how could Black satisfactorily decline this gambit?

A 3...♘b8-c6 would be useless as after 4 c3xd4, White has a lovely pawn centre. Black could throw a spanner in White's development works with 3...d4-d3 or hit out immediately with 3...d7-d5. Nevertheless the most common way to decline is 3...♘g8-f6. As White wants his bishop on c4, 4 ♗f1-d3, to look after the e-pawn, would not be good, and so 4 e4-e5 is best. Then after 4...♘f6-d5, play has transposed into the aforementioned Sicilian 2 c3 variation (more commonly arrived at by 1 e2-e4 c7-c5 2 c2-c3 ♘g8-f6 3 e4-e5 ♘f6-d5 4 d2-d4 c5xd4).

4 Application of rules to create theory: 1 e2-e4 Openings

27) The Italian Game

1	e2-e4	e7-e5
2	♘g1-f3	♘b8-c6
3	♗f1-c4 *(107)*	

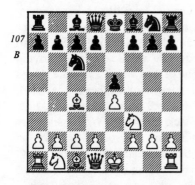

Undoubtedly the most common opening amongst novices is the Italian Game, also called the 'Giuoco Piano'. In under-11 years tournaments, it is not unusual for the above position to crop up in well over 50% of the games. Indeed some of the individual players may well have this position in every game in, for instance, a six-round tournament (i.e. with White and Black). It would, however, be ridiculous to label this a beginner's opening as it is played at all levels, including on occasion World Champions Anatoly Karpov and Garry Kasparov.

As Black is eager to get castled, it is logical that his next move will be with a kingside minor piece. Hence the two main candidates are:

> A: 3...♗f8-c5
> B: 3...♘g8-f6

Although clearly distinguishable, it is quite possible that these two lines will transpose.

A: 3 ... ♗f8-c5 *(108)*

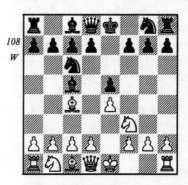

Now it is White who must make a decision, even if it is not a critical one. He could castle or play 4 d2-d3, and 4 ♘b1-c3 isn't that bad. Nevertheless White is more likely to want to try for a pawn break.

4 c2-c3

Black can now see d2-d4 coming and won't want to fall in with White's plans of getting a big centre. Hence the casual 4...d7-d6 doesn't hit the mark in view of 5 d2-d4 when unfortunately 5...e5xd4 6 c3xd4 is forced since 5....♗c5-b6 loses a pawn to 6 d4xe5. However this plan of maintaining a strong-point on e5 might be achieved with 4...♕d8-e7. This attempts to dissuade d2-d4 as the e4-pawn will be attacked, and the whole idea is only possible as ♘b1-c3-d5 is not legal. If then 5 0-0 (ultimately hoping to embarrass the black queen and king on the e-file), 5...d7-d6 6 d2-d4 ♗c5-b6 is feasible since the queens will not be opposed. This resulting position may be slightly better for White, but he should resist the temptation of the space-gaining, but bishop-limiting 7 d4-d5. The centre is blocked and in such a closed position, Black will not be worried about being behind in development.

4 ...   ♘g8-f6

Another way of taking advantage of the fact that the b1 knight can't develop on c3. Black attacks the e4-pawn, again trying to put White off the idea of 5 d2-d4 although this is a tactical possibility. For example 5...e5xd4 *(109)* and now:

109
W

a) 6 c3xd4 ♗c5-b4+. Now White can play safe with 7 ♗c1-d2 ♗b4xd2+ 8 ♘b1xd2. Threatening 9 e4-e5, he appears to have a comfortable edge, but in fact Black can equalize with 8...d7-d5!, removing one of the two central white pawns and leaving the other one isolated. 7 ♘b1-c3 is a more tricky old line. Black cannot let White get away with this and so has to enter the critical variation 7...♘f6xe4 8 0-0, when he must be very careful. Greed is punished after 8...♘e4xc3?! 9 b2xc3 ♗b4xc3 10 ♕d1-b3! ♗c3xa1 11 ♗c4xf7+ ♔e8-f8 12 ♗c1-g5 ♘c6-e7 13 ♘f3-e5, with a devastating attack. Instead 8...♗b4xc3 9 d4-d5 (complicating things rather than settling for the better for Black 9 b2xc3 d7-d5) 9...♗c3-f6 10 ♖f1-e1 ♘c6-e7 11 ♖e1xe4 d7-d6 is more accurate, when Black will probably suffer a little discomfort for his extra pawn.

b) 6 e4-e5 d7-d5! (often this move, though not easy to see, is the best and indeed the only real reply to e4-e5) 7 ♗c4-b5 ♘f6-e4 8 c3xd4 ♗c5-b6 with chances for both sides. The e5-pawn might be a tower of strength, but the d4-pawn is a definite target.

5 d2-d3

White's d2-d4 has been put on ice, but this is not a disaster for him. The pawn on c3 controls the d4-square and facilitates a possible queenside expansion with b2-b4 and a2-a4. While many may argue that the queen's knight has been deprived of its natural developing square, in fact it has plenty of other long-term options such as ♘b1-d2-f1-g3-f5!.

B: 3 ... ♘g8-f6 *(110)*

White's e4-pawn is attacked and he should not ignore this unless he wants to enter another tactical variation such as 4 d2-d4 e5xd4 5 0-0 *(111)* (if 5 e4-e5 then again 5...d7-d5!). Then there are two continuations, both with some slightly crazy lines:

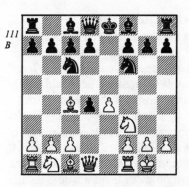

a) 5...♘f6xe4 6 ♖f1-e1 d7-d5 7 ♗c4xd5 ♕d8xd5 8 ♘b1-c3 ♕d5-a5 9 ♘c3xe4 or 7 ♘b1-c3 d5xc4 8 ♖e1xe4+ ♗f8-e7 9 ♘f3xd4, with dynamic equality in both cases.

b) 5...♗f8-c5 6 e4-e5 d7-d5! 7 e5xf6 d5xc4 8 ♖f1-e1+ ♗c8-e6. Black's has the bishop pair and strong central pawns to compensate for his currently awkward king and a potential lack of kingside pawns.

After 3...♘g8-f6 we have already seen earlier in the book how 4 ♘b1-c3?! allows 4...♘f6xe4!, but I feel that a few words should be said about 4 d2-d3. After 4...♗f8-c5, 5 c2-c3 would of course transpose into (A).

It is not wise for White to put all his eggs in one basket with the ♗c1-g5 and ♘b1-c3-d5 trick, although many beginners (particularly juniors) do so. Take a couple of hypothetical examples:

a) 5 ♘b1-c3 d7-d6 6 ♗c1-g5 h7-h6 7 ♗g5-h4 ♗c8-e6. If White now doubles Black's pawns with 8 ♗c4xe6 f7xe6, then Black will have a useful half-open f-file, and if 8 0-0 instead, then Black may try 9...g7-g5. This may weaken his kingside, but with ...♕d8-e7 and ...0-0-0 in mind he could easily find himself with a good attack.

b) 5 0-0 d7-d6 6 ♗c1-g5?! (at present this move would not fit in well with c2-c3 ideas, where it would not yet be clear what the bishop's destination would be and so the bishop ought not be moved) 6...h7-h6 7 ♗g5-h4 g7-g5 8 ♗h4-g3 h5-h4 (the start of a beautiful concept) 9 ♘f3xg5 (moving the h-pawn to give the g3-bishop some air would only result in accelerating Black's attack) 9...h5-h4 10 ♘g5xf7 h4xg3! 11 ♘f7xd8 ♗c8-g4 12 ♕d1-d2 ♘c6-d4 13 ♘b1-c3 (preventing 13...♘d4-e2+ and ...♖h8xh2 mate, but ...) 13...♘d4-f3+ 14 g2xf3 ♗g4xf3 and checkmate is unstoppable.

4 ♘f3-g5

This is the other alternative. It doesn't really deserve to work since it blatantly breaks an opening guideline. This is, however, an acceptable variation, which makes it very popular amongst those searching for an easy win.

4 ... d7-d5

Blocking the white bishop's view of f7. Dangerous for unprepared white players is 4...♗f8-c5 (the 'Wilkes-Barre' or 'Traxler' variation) intending 5 ♘g5xf7 (5 ♗c4xf7+ is safer) 5...♗c5xf2+ with a nifty counter-attack.

5 e4xd5 *(112)*

112
B

Now follows what is probably the hardest continuation for the reader to understand, and indeed for me to explain. Here 5...♘f6xd5 is bad, not necessarily because of the speculative 6 ♘g5xf7 ♔e8xf7 7 ♕d1-f3+ ♔f7-e6 (the 'Fried Liver'), but rather 6 d2-d4! e5xd4 (if 6...♘c6xd4 then 7 c2-c3 wins a piece) 7 0-0 with two possibilities, both decisively in White's favour:

a) 7...♗f8-e7 8 ♘g5xf7! ♔e8xf7 9 ♕d1-h5+ ♔f7-e6 (losing quickly but the alternatives are all pretty bleak) 10 ♖f1-e1+ ♔e6-d6 11 ♕h5xd5 mate.

b) 7...♗c8-e6 8 ♖f1-e1 ♕d8-d7 9 ♘g5xf7!! (absolutely beautiful as at first sight it appears that Black can take this knight in either of three ways) 9...♔e8xf7 (in fact 9...♗e6xf7 is illegal and 9...♕d7xf7 loses to 10 ♗c4xd5) 10 ♕d1-f3+ ♔f7-g6 11 ♖e1xe6+ ♕d7xe6 12 ♗c4-d3+ also mates.

5 ... ♘c6-a5

Knights on the rim are dim, but this one has a purpose. Black seeks to remove White's light-squared bishop from the a2-g8 diagonal. If now White were to retreat the bishop to, say, e2, then Black could happily play 6...♘f6xd5 as the heat is off his f7-pawn. The knight would look silly on a5, but it could soon return to c6 after a job well done.

    6 ♗c4-b5+   c7-c6
    7 d5xc6   b7xc6 *(113)*

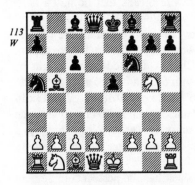

113
W

Black has an apparently offside knight and two isolated queenside pawns. Despite this, he has reasonable compensation for his pawn as White is behind in development and those pieces which are out, are being hassled.

    8 ♗b5-e2

If White retreats the bishop to a4, then Black can take advantage of White's two loose pieces after 8...h7-h6 9 ♘g5-f3 e5-e4 10 ♘f3-e5, with the fork 10...♕d8-d4!.

    8 ...   h7-h6
    9 ♘g5-f3   e5-e4

    10 ♘f3-e5   ♗f8-d6

White has kept an extra pawn, but Black's pieces are active, and he has good chances on the kingside.

28) The Ruy Lopez

    1 e2-e4   e7-e5
    2 ♘g1-f3   ♘b8-c6
    3 ♗f1-b5 *(114)*

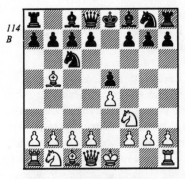

114
B

White develops the king's bishop in order to prepare a quick 0-0. Although pressurizing the c6-knight, White need not intend exchanging his bishop for this knight unless the circumstances are particularly favourable. However, it is clear that the knight is protecting the e5-pawn, which is being attacked by White's f3-knight, so the big question is whether White is actually threatening to win a pawn.

    3 ...   a7-a6!

This move implies not. Black puts the question to the white bishop, the idea being that should White retreat, at Black could at any stage throw in ...b7-b5 removing the ♗b5xc6 possibility altogether. It seems illogical for White to bring the bishop back to c4, as a hole on a7 is nothing (in fact ...a7-a6 is quite useful) and hence 3 ♗f1-c4 should have been played in the first place. Thus White has two main alternatives:

> A: 4 ♗b5xc6
> B: 4 ♗b5-a4

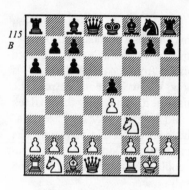

115
B

A: 4 ♗b5xc6

Known as the 'Exchange Variation'.

4 ...   d7xc6

Recapture towards the centre is one rule (more applicable to outside pawns), but here Black is doing himself more favours by freeing his bishop and queen. The latter is especially relevant if White tries to grab the e-pawn: 5 ♘f3xe5?! is foiled by 5...♕d8-d4! 6 ♘e5-f3 ♕d4xe4+. Putting the queen in front of the king is not dangerous here as White cannot castle out of check and spring a ♖f1-e1 on Black. Indeed, after 7 ♕d1-e2 ♕e4xe2+ 8 ♔e1xe2, Black is better since he has the advantage of the two bishops in an open position (approaching an endgame).

5 0-0 *(115)*

Now threatening 6 ♘f3xe5 for sure. This could also be said of ♘b1-c3, against which Black would have a similar selection of moves to the main text.

The fact that Black has doubled pawns means that he has a half-open file as well as extra control over a key central square (d5). A way for White to try to exploit Black's doubled pawns might be with 5 d2-d4 since after 5...e5xd4 6 ♕d1xd4 ♕d8xd4 7 ♘f3xd4 Black has an ineffective queenside majority (with White having a clear pawn plus on the kingside). However as previously stated, Black has the perfect complement in the two bishops and all he needs to do is undouble his c-pawns (e.g. trade one off), to hold the upper hand.

5 ...   ♗c8-g4

Black indirectly defends the e-pawn by means of a pin. This is by no means the only move, with 5...♗f8-d6 (bishops don't like just to defend pawns, but this bishop will see better days later in the game), 5...f7-f6 (not exposing the king as White's light-squared bishop is gone for good), and 5...♕d8-d6 (the black queen is not in a vulnerable position here) are all quite reasonable.

6 h2-h3

White hopes to obtain a slight advantage due to having a good versus a bad bishop after 6...♗g4xf3 7 ♕d1xf3.

6 ...   h7-h5!? *(116)*

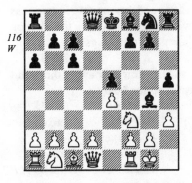

116
W

This may come as a shock! Black is, to say the least, unsubtle and it is clear that he is seeking excitement for his rook along the h-file. For example, if now 7 h3xg4 h5xg4 8 ♘f3xe5, then 8...♕d8-h4 (with the queen and rook combining to threaten 8...♕h4-h1 mate) 9 f2-f3 g4-g3 leads to a forced checkmate. White is therefore advised to ignore the bishop for the time being with 7 d2-d3, but Black can continue aggressively with moves like ...♕d8-f6, ...♗f8-c5, ...♘g8-e7-g6, and ...0-0-0. It is fair to say that from the illustrated position, for a Ruy Lopez Exchange Variation, play would be untypically entertaining.

B: 4 ♗b5-a4 *(117)*

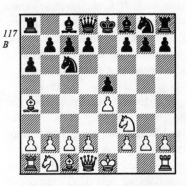

117
B

4 ...   ♘g8-f6

Black could play 4...b7-b5 immediately, but it has already been established that 4 ♗b5xc6 was not too dangerous, so why should White fear 5 ♗a4xc6? It's interesting that after 4...b7-b5 5 ♗a4-b3, play has transposed to an Italian Game but with Black's pawns on a6 and b5, and White's bishop on b3 instead of c4. This probably favours White, although the 'Norwegian Variation', 5...♘c6-a5 (knights on the rim are dim, but this one is tracking White's light-squared bishop), aims to prove otherwise. Note after 6 ♘f3xe5?! ♘a5xb3 7 a2xb3 (White has lost a bishop for a knight, but gained a half-open a-file and some control of the c4-square), not for the first time we would see 7...♕d8-g5, winning the pawn back.

5 0-0

White is not too worried about 5...♘f6xe4 (the 'Open Lopez') as he will hope to catch the black king in the centre with 6 ♖f1-e1 or perhaps 6 d2-d4 first. Besides, White is also not too keen on playing ♘b1-c3 since (like in the Italian Game), he may be intending c2-c3 with or without d2-d4 to follow.

5 ...   ♗f8-e7

This doesn't exactly appear to be the most adventurous square for the bishop, but here it is out of harm's way (on c5 it would have been vulnerable to the aforementioned c2-c3 and d2-d4 break). It also performs the useful function of shielding the king before it is castled, so that 6 ♗a4xc6 d7xc6 7 ♘f3xe5 ♘f6xe4 is no problem for him (a pin against the king might have been awkward).

6 ♖f1-e1   b7-b5

Necessary now since after 6...0-0, White can win a pawn with 7 ♗a4xc6 d7xc6 8 ♘f3xe5.

7 ♗a4-b3   0-0 *(118)*

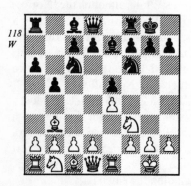

118
W

8 c2-c3

White prepares 9 d2-d4 although 8 d2-d4 immediately is also possible. The text move is straight to the

point, but it allows the fascinating 'Marshall Attack'. It is because of this aggressive possibility for Black that White often prefers other lines (known as Anti-Marshall systems). Two such moves are the solid 8 d2-d3 (though with c2-c3 in mind for later) and 8 a2-a4 (seeking to demonstrate Black's advanced queenside pawns as weak and/or introduce the a1-rook into the proceedings).

8 ...   d7-d5!?

Sacrificing a pawn, the solid safer option being 8...d7-d6.

9 e4xd5	**♘f6xd5**
10 ♘f3xe5	**♘c6xe5**
11 ♖e1xe5	**c7-c6**
12 d2-d4	**♗e7-d6**
13 ♖e5-e1	**♕d8-h4** *(119)*

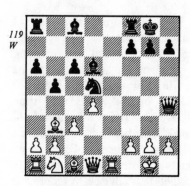

119
W

For his pawn deficit, Black has a nice attack. In fact although Black still has more troops to bring in, he already has enough pieces trained on the white king so as to make one slip-up fatal. For instance here, White must play 14 g2-g3 as 14 h2-h3? loses to 14...♗c8xh3! 15

g2xh3 ♕h4xh3, e.g. 16 ♗b3xd5
♗d6-h2+ 17 ♔g1-h1 ♗h2-g3+ 18
♔h1-g1 ♕h3-h2+ 19 ♔g1-f1
♕h2xf2 mate.

29) The French Defence

1 e2-e4	e7-e6
2 d2-d4	d7-d5 *(120)*

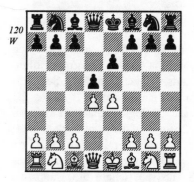

120
W

How should White handle this
opening? Well, it is clear that he
must deal with the threat of
3...d5xe4 and hence 3 e4-e5 and 3
e4xd5 stand out immediately. The
former is dealt with in the main
text, but the latter only deserves a
few words. The problem piece for
Black in the French Defence is the
'bad' c8-bishop. If White can keep
it devoid of activity throughout the
game, then at the very least he will
have excellent chances in the
endgame. After 4 e4xd5 e6xd5,
this bishop has already been freed
and as the position is symmetrical,
White is left with only the minor
(in this position anyway) advantage of being the one to move.

Although pawn moves are a beginners instinctive reaction, it soon
becomes apparent that in fact
White could also do well simply to
defend his e4-pawn with a piece
(as was seen earlier, 3 f2-f3 is bad
as this pawn could not recapture on
e4 anyhow due to a check on h4).
However queen moves are out and
it is for the same 'too valuable'
reason that 3 ♗f1-d3 (knights before bishops) is not good, i.e.
3...d5xe4 4 ♗d3xe4 ♘g8-f6 when
to preserve itself, the bishop must
move for a third consecutive time.

Hence the alternative moves are
with the b1-knight. If we assume
that White's e-pawn could easily
be tempted to e5, then Black's
kingside pieces may be stuck for
space. After 3 ♘b1-c3, rather than
fighting with the g8-knight over
the e7-square, Black's king's bsi-
hop can exert further pressure on
the centre with the pin 3...♗f8-b4
(the 'Winawer Variation'). As this
renews the threat of the pawn-win-
ning ...d5xe4, White generally
now opts for 4 e4-e5 *(121)*.

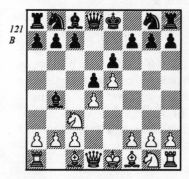

121
B

With the centre blocked (and the fixed pawns leaving White with a clear space advantage), one good idea for Black here is to make a pawn break and secure some room for his queenside pieces, with 4...c7-c5. White must then be careful not to lose his d4-pawn (followed by his e5-pawn) as ultimately it would then be Black with the big pawn centre! White would like a pawn to support d4 and he has just the way of getting one to perform such a function: 5 a2-a3 ♗b4xc3+ 6 b2xc3 – by no means the only continuation of the 'French Winawer', but a very popular one. White has a strong pawn centre, in return for some structural weaknesses on the queenside. By exchanging off a minor piece, Black has more room to play with, but he has lost a good bishop and must be careful to keep an eye on his dark squares. To avoid the pin, White can also try 3 ♘b1-d2 *(122)* (the 'French Tarrasch'). This temporarily obstructs the c1-bishop, but not the c2-pawn, and when played at top levels, play usually continues in one of the following three ways:

a) 3...♘b8-c6 4 ♘g1-f3 ♘g8-f6 5 e4-e5 ♘f6-d7, when being rather cramped, Black must shortly make the freeing pawn break ...f7-f6.

b) 3...♘g8-f6 4 e4-e5 ♘f6-d7, when Black will soon strike out at White's centre with ...c7-c5 and possibly later with ...f7-f6 as well.

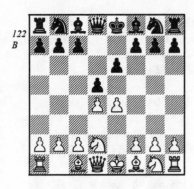

122 B

c) 3...c7-c5. Played before the centre is blocked, this move often leads to Black being saddled with an isolated d-pawn. If this is the case, the logic is that the knight on d2 is not on the right track to pressurize the d5-pawn. i.e. 3...c7-c5 wouldn't have been playable after 3 ♘b1-c3, where the knight attacks what would be an isolated pawn – in the short time that it remains on the board!

Note that whether White plays 3 ♘b1-c3 or 3 ♘b1-d2, Black does have the possibility of 3...d5xe4 4 ♘c3(or d2)xe4. Then with freedom of movement for all of his pieces and a further advanced centre pawn (generally the two come hand in hand), White is obviously better although Black has no weaknesses and can adopt a solid piece formation.

We shall now look at the 'Advance Variation':

3 e4-e5   c7-c5

Almost certainly the best move. Black targets White's d4-pawn (which supports his e5-pawn) and buys his pieces some more space. We have seen the grim repercussions of leaving this pawn break out in Section 17 where alternatively Black chose to move (but not exactly develop) his pieces rather aimlessly and then got horribly crushed by a Greek Gift sacrifice.

4 c2-c3 *(123)*

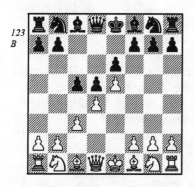

123
B

The natural response is for White to support the d4-pawn, although the text move does remove the c3-square from the white knight.

4 ...   ♘b8-c6
5 ♘g1-f3

Section 20 showed us that, although giving support to the e5-pawn, 5 f2-f4 restricts the c1-bishop and, particularly in view of a later ...♘g8-h6-f5, is definitely surplus to requirements.

5 ...   ♕d8-b6

Exerting further pressure on d4 and through it to f2, while also tying the c1-bishop down to the protection of the b2-pawn.

6 ♗f1-e2 *(124)*

Due to Greek gifts and other attacking possibilities, White really wants to put this bishop on d3. In fact he can do so, since 6...c5xd4 7 c3xd4 ♘c6xd4?? 8 ♘f3xd4 ♕b6xd4?? loses a queen to 9 ♗d3-b5+. However, if instead Black interpolates 7...♗c8-d7 White does have problems defending his d4-pawn, since there are no longer any light-squared bishop checks available. In fact, the only satisfactory solution is to sacrifice it (if 8 ♗d3-c2 then 8...♘c6-b4 and Black's 'bad' bishop is likely to become quite good on b5) with 8 0-0 (the 'Milner-Barry Gambit') 8...♘c6xd4 9 ♘f3xd4 ♕b6xd4 10 ♘b1-c3 (or 10 ♕d1-e2) when White gets some active piece compensation for the pawn(s) (though whether it is enough is debatable).

The 'will-he-or-won't-he-swap' tension on c5 and d4 is quite annoying for White and so another possibility is 6 a2-a3. The idea behind this is to force the issue with 7 b2-b4. Normally Black should be reluctant to close up the position, but now he may consider 6...c5-c4 as the b3-square looks ripe for occupation. Then his king will be safer on the queenside and so he should be looking to play ...0-0-0.

124
B

6 ...   ♘g8-e7

Now Black's cards are on the table. He intends to trade pawns on d4 and then play ...♘e7-f5. White needs to come up with a defender for his d-pawn in two moves. Were Black to play 6...♘g8-h6 instead, then White could fall back on a queen-trapping tactic: 7 ♗c1xh6 ♕b6xb2 (White is slightly better after 7...g7xh6, but should avoid conceding dark-squared holes with moves like 8 b2-b3, preferring 8 ♕d1-d2 instead) 8 ♗h6-e3 ♕b2xa1 9 ♕d1-c2 with 0-0 and ♘b1-d2 to follow.

After 6...c5xd4 7 c3xd4 ♘g8-h6, this tactic fails but instead the c3-square is now vacant and so White has 8 ♘b1-c3 ♘h6-f5 9 ♘c3-a4 (or 9 ♗e2-b5) drawing the black queen away from its attack on d4.

7 ♘b1-a3   ♘e7-f5
8 ♘a3-c2

Just in the nick of time! White is at full stretch to protect his d4-pawn, but aims slowly to push Black back. After 8...c5xd4 9 c3xd4, a couple of lines run:

a) 8...♗f8-b4+ 9 ♔e1-f1. Necessary, as alternatives lose the d-pawn, and besides White can castle by hand (i.e. with g2-g3 or g3-g4 and ♔f1-g2). Black must also be careful now since, for example, 9...0-0? 10 g2-g4 ♘f5-e7 loses a piece to 11 a2-a3.

b) 8...♗f8-e7 9 0-0 ♗c8-d7 10 ♗e2-d3 preparing a timely removal of the f5-knight and setting a devious trap: 10...♘f5xd4? 11 ♘f3xd4 ♘c6xd4 12 ♗c1-e3 ♗e7-c5 13 b2-b4 winning a piece.

5 Application of rules to create theory: 1 d2-d4 Openings

30) The Queen's Gambit Accepted

1 d2-d4	d7-d5
2 c2-c4	d5xc4 *(125)*

125
W

The Queen's Gambit has been mentioned on numerous occasions throughout this book and the first new thing that the reader is about to discover here is that it isn't really a genuine gambit. It appears as though White has made a pawn break (2 c2-c4) and in compensation for a sacrificed pawn, he now has a free rein in the centre. In fact in either of the two variations below, it is clear that White can easily regain his pawn and any futile efforts by Black to keep the c4-pawn merely compromise his po-

sition. Below are two possible ways of playing against the 'QGA':

    A: 3 e2-e4
    B: 3 ♘g1-f3

A: 3 e2-e4

Straight to the point. White takes complete control of the centre and immediately threatens to regain the sacrificed pawn. Indeed if Black tried to hang on to it with 3...b7-b5?!, then White would do best to undermine and chip away at this tenuous defence. Hence 4 a2-a4 starts the ball rolling and if 4...c7-c6 (4...a7-a6 will never be much use as the a6-pawn will be pinned anyway), then 5 b2-b3. After 5...c4xb3 6 a4xb5 c6xb5 7 ♗f1xb5+, with 8 ♕d1xb3 to follow, White will have regained his pawn with interest (i.e. still the nice centre, but now also with pressure against Black's isolated a7-pawn).

As a junior I played (and indeed still do play) the Queen's Gambit. If my opponents took on c4, then I would reply with 3 e2-e4. However after a while I was informed that this is a mistake and so I switched to the system described in (B). Approximately ten years later though I discovered that I had been misinformed and so returned to my old favourite, bitter that I had missed out on a decade's experience. The truth then is that 3 e2-e4 is perfectly playable, but if Black plays accurately, possibly not as good as it looks at first sight.

3 ...   ♘g8-f6

Moves such as 3...e7-e6 are way too passive and as alternatives to the text, Black should be looking to strike out in the centre with either 3...c7-c5 or 3...e7-e5. Note after 3...e7-e5, White has no advantage whatsoever after 4 d4xe5?! ♕d8xd1+ 5 ♚e1xd1 as the e5-pawn is as weak as the c4-pawn. Also 4 d4-d5 allows Black to occupy a nice diagonal with 4...♗f8-c5 and so 4 ♘g1-f3 e5xd4 5 ♗f1xc4 is correct. If White does not win back the d4-pawn, then he will gain tremendous counterplay against f7.

4 e4-e5

More natural-looking is 4 ♘b1-c3, but then Black has 4...e7-e5! with the previous gambit continuation no longer being available.

4 ...   ♘f6-d5

5 ♗f1xc4 *(126)*

Black has a useful outpost on d5 and the chance to build up some pressure on White's d4-pawn, while White has that handy cramping and attacking weapon, a pawn on e5.

126
B

5 ...   ♘d5-b6

6 ♗c4-b3

6 ♗c4-d3 is also reasonable since 6...♕d8xd4?? loses the queen to 7 ♗d3-b5+.

6 ...   ♘b8-c6

The position is evenly poised. Incredibly, a forced draw can be reached after 7 ♘g1-f3 ♗c8-g4 8 ♘f3-g5 (8 ♗b3xf7+ ♚e8xf7 9 ♘f3-g5+ ♚f7-e8 10 ♕d1xg4 is unclear because of 10...♕d8xd4) 8...♗g4xd1 9 ♗b3xf7+ ♚e8-d7 10 ♗f7-e6+ ♚d7-e8 11 ♗e6-f7+ etc. Alternatively then White can play 7 ♘g1-e2 (so as to avoid the pin, like in the French Tarrasch as we saw in the previous chapter) or 7 ♗c1-e3.

B: 3 ♘g1-f3   ♘g8-f6

4 e2-e3 *(127)*

A more cautious approach. Again, the c4-pawn is as good as in the bag as 4...b7-b5 will receive the same treatment as before: 5 a2-a4 c7-c6 6 b2-b3. Although the e-pawn stops at e3 now, White will have it in mind to advance to e4 later when he is better developed and thus less prone to Black's central thrusts.

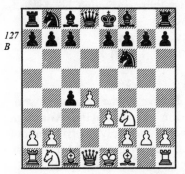

127
B

4 ... &c8-g4

An old continuation, with which Black gets his bishop outside the pawn chain before playing ...e7-e6. Alternatively Black could deploy it on b7 following ...a7-a6 and if possible ...b7-b5. In this case there would be no objection to playing an early ...e7-e6 and challenging White's centre with ...c7-c5.

5 &f1xc4 *(128)*

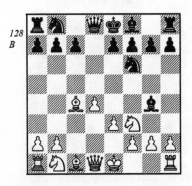

128
B

It should be observed here that White has three big threats:

a) 6 &d1-b3 hitting both the b7- and f7-pawns.

b) 6 &c4xf7+ &e8xf7 7 &f3-e5+ &f7-e8 8 &e5xg4 winning a pawn and preventing Black from castling.

c) 6 &f3-e5 when 6...&g4xd1 could be adequately met by 7 &c4xf7 mate and 6...&g4-h5 by 7 &d1xh5!.

5 ... **e7-e6**

Unfortunately Black's most obvious reply puts a stop to them all!

6 h2-h3 **&g4-h5**

Not surprisingly, Black isn't keen on parting with his bishop (for a knight anyway).

7 &b1-c3

White's extra centre pawn gives him a slight advantage, but while he will be aiming for e3-e4, Black will be getting ready to hit White with either ...c7-c5 or even ...e6-e5.

31) The Queen's Gambit Declined

1 d2-d4 **d7-d5**
2 c2-c4 **e7-e6**

If Black is going to turn down White's temporary offer, then he must be sure to bolster d5 sufficiently so as to keep a pawn there (and thus a white pawn out of e4). Therefore 2...&g8-f6 is inadequate because of 3 c4xd5 &d8xd5 4 &b1-c3 or 3...&f6xd5 4 &g1-f3 followed by e2-e4.

Another popular method of declining the gambit is the 'Slav Defence', 2...c6. This has the advantage of not blocking in the c8-bishop, although when contemplating such a move as ...♗c8-f5, Black should beware of the ♕d1-b3 possibility for White (hitting both d5 and b7).

  3 ♘b1-c3 ♘g8-f6 *(129)*

The long term result of 3...c7-c5 (the 'Tarrasch Defence') is likely to be an isolated d-pawn for Black after 4 c4xd5 e6xd5, although with 4...c5xd4 (the 'Hennig-Schara'), Black really does gambit a pawn for some activity himself, i.e. 5 ♕d1xd4 ♘b8-c6 6 ♕d4-d1 e6xd5 7 ♕d1xd5 ♗c8-d7.

Adding further immediate pawn support to the centre with 3...c7-c6 can lead to the 'Semi-Slav' after 4 ♘g1-f3 ♘g8-f6 but allows White the possibility of 4 e2-e4. The specific move order here is partly designed to avoid the rather tedious 'Exchange Variation' of the 'Slav Defence' (2...c7-c6 3 c4xd5 c6xd5) and the variation in (A) below.

From the diagram, play now divides into lines in which White clarifies the situation on c4 and d5, and those in which he doesn't. Hence:

A: 4 c4xd5
B: 4 ♘g1-f3

A: 4 c4xd5

Known as the 'Exchange variation' of the QGD. Although White is rarely worried about ...d5xc4, White opts to trade now anyway. One reason for this is to make Black decide now which way to recapture.

  4 ... e6xd5

4...♘f6xd5 can lead to the 'Semi-Tarrasch' after 5 e2-e4 ♘d5xc3 6 b2xc3 c7-c5 7 ♘g1-f3, when after 7...c5xd4 8 c3xd4, it is a question of which is better, White's big pawn centre in the opening/middlegame or, if Black survives, his queenside pawn majority in the endgame.

  5 ♗c1-g5 *(130)*

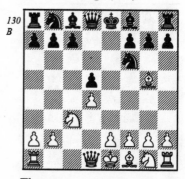

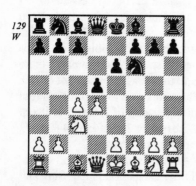

There are two common errors made by Black in the QGD. The

first is the habit of playing ...♗c8-e6, for example now in order to facilitate ...♘b8-d7 without 'blocking this bishop in'. In fact this can be categorized as moving a piece rather than developing it. The bishop on e6 does nothing useful and is actually detrimental in that it is an unwanted obstacle on Black's half-open e-file. The bishop on c8 defends the b7-pawn and should only come out when it has somewhere good to go.

Slightly more basic is that occasionally the mistake is made of playing ...♘b8-c6. In Queen's Pawn openings, c-pawns inevitably play a key role. The c7-pawn may wish to eventually attack White's centre with ...c7-c5 or just support Black's own with ...c7-c6. In addition a black knight on c6 performs no particularly useful function (on d7 it is more easily transferable to the kingside).

5 ...   ♘b8-d7

White was prepared to concede a bishop for a knight (6 ♗g5xf6) in order to double Black's pawns (if 6...♕d8xf6 then 7 ♘c3xd5). The text move prevents this and sets a devious trap. If now 6 ♘c3xd5?, Black can temporarily sacrifice his queen with 6...♘f6xd5! 7 ♗g5xd8 ♗f8-b4+ 8 ♕d1-d2 ♗b4xd2+ 9 ♔e1xd2 ♔e8xd8, something that many years ago I for one fell for.

Also very reasonable (and likely to transpose) are 5...c7-c6 and 5...♗f8-e7, although once again,

the latter not with the continuation of 6 e2-e3 ♗c8-f5?! because of 7 ♗g5xf6 ♗e7xf6 8 ♕d1-b3! winning a pawn.

6 e2-e3

Now threatening 7 ♘c3xd5 as in the above variation White could play ♔e1-e2 rather than blocking the bishop check on b4 with his queen.

6 ...   c7-c6
7 ♗f1-d3 *(131)*

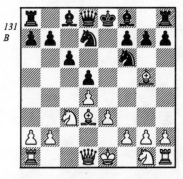

131
B

'Knights before bishops' is a rule only because more often than not the bishops have more options. White knows that he wants a bishop on d3, but is possibly less sure about where to post his g1-knight.

7 ...   ♗f8-e7

Despite plenty of current protection for the f6-knight, it is necessary to deploy the dark-squared bishop here in order to unpin it. Later on in the game it may be OK to nudge it on to the more aggressive placing, d6.

8 ♕d1-c2

Keeping Black guessing about where the g1-knight is bound for as well as which side White will castle. A reason for 7...♗f8-e7 is highlighted now. If the black bishop were on d6, then Black would be unable to castle in view of ♗d3xh7+. As the reader will soon see, one common plan for Black is to manoeuvre his d7-knight to g6 (via f8). It would not be safe there if it weren't protected by both the h-pawn and the f-pawn and so Black should not be too trigger-happy about ...h7-h6.

| 8 ... | 0-0 |
| 9 ♘g1-e2 | ♖f8-e8 (132) |

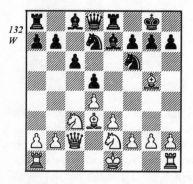

132
W

A standard starting position of the QGD Exchange Variation. White can castle kingside and launch a minority attack (rolling his own queenside pawns down the board so as to weaken Black's) or he can castle queenside and launch an assault on the black king. Generally Black's main play should be on the opposite side of the board to White, thus making

for a very exciting game. The manoeuvre ...♘d7-f8-g6 will then be more applicable if White castles kingside (i.e. with a black attack in mind) and Black may also choose to utilize his unpinning bishop with ...♘f6-e4 (probably with the previously condemned ...h7-h6, ♗g5-h4 thrown in), which despite initial appearances, doesn't lose a pawn.

B: | 4 ♘g1-f3 | ♘b8-d7 |
| 5 ♗c1-g5 (133) | |

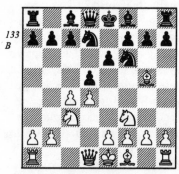

133
B

Although this is the most aggressive square for White's dark-squared bishop (as it helps to exert pressure on the black d5-pawn), it is quite acceptable for White to move it to f4 instead. With the bishop on g5 or f4, there are are a variety of set-ups that Black can adopt. One idea is for him to fianchetto his bishop on b7, although in the following text, Black prefers to bolster the centre with a pawn.

| 5 ... | c7-c6 |
| 6 e2-e3 | |

It is not too late for White to transpose to the 'Exchange variation' with 6 c4xd5, although this time his king's knight will be on the perfectly reasonable f3-square rather than e2. Note that on f3, the knight has e5 to go to, whereas on e2, it might zap to f4 or g3.

6 ...   ♕d8-a5

Now it *is* too late! In this 'Cambridge Springs' variation, Black swings his queen out to the fairly safe square a5 in order to pressurize White's c3 knight. If now 7 c4xd5, then Black would recapture with his knight and the previously delayed deployment of his dark-squared bishop would be justified as it zooms straight to b4. Note that in all Queen's Gambit lines Black should be reluctant to part with his dark-squared bishop for a knight (explaining why there was no point moving it to b4 in (A)). Here though White would be faced with some problems, since, being outside the pawn chain, his own bishop is of no use in the defence.

7 ♗f1-d3? *(134)*

134
B

A natural enough move, but under-estimating Black's play against both his c3-knight and what will be a fairly loose g5-bishop.

Much better are 7 ♗g5xf6 (removing one of White's problems) and 7 ♘f3-d2 (unpinning the c3-knight). It should be remarked at this stage that in all lines except the text (where he wins material), Black must consider what he is going to do with his c8-bishop which in contrast to the 'Exchange Variation', has no obvious way out (aiming for a later ...e6-e5 is one possibility).

7 ...   ♘f6-e4!

And already White is objectively lost. What White would have overlooked here is that after 8 ♕d1-c2, 8...♘e4xg5 9 ♘f3xg5 d5xc4 wins a piece as the g5-knight is hanging.

32) The Nimzo-Indian Defence

1 d2-d4   ♘g8-f6

Black prevents White dominating the centre wuth 2 e2-e4.

2 c2-c4

White knows that in order to obtain the aforementioned e2-e4 he must also hinder Black's ...d7-d5. The golden rule of not obstructing the c-pawn in Queen's Pawn openings applies very much here; as we have already seen, after 2 ♘b1-c3 d7-d5, it is exceedingly difficult for White to achieve a pawn break.

2 ...   e7-e6

3 ♘b1-c3

It is of course reasonable for White to avoid the forthcoming pin with other sensible moves such as 3 ♘g1-f3. However, the text move is the most forcing continuation as it gets straight to the point in threatening 4 e2-e4.

3 ...   ♗f8-b4 *(135)*

Initiating the 'Nimzo-Indian Defence', although with 3...d7-d5, Black could alternatively transpose to the Queen's Gambit Declined.

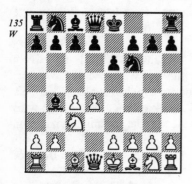

From here on, White can either continue forcefully, consistently trying to achieve e2-e4 or else, for the time being at least, simply develop. Let us take a brief look at no less than nine fairly common fourth move possibilities for White:

A: 4 a2-a3
B: 4 f2-f3
C: 4 ♗c1-g5
D: 4 g2-g3

E: 4 e2-e3
F: 4 ♕d1-c2
G: 4 ♕d1-b3
H: 4 ♘g1-f3
I: 4 ♗c1-d2

A: 4 a2-a3

Some of these lines have names. This is called the 'Sämisch Variation' (we already know that there is a Sämisch Variation against the King's Indian Defence).

4 ...   ♗b4xc3+

It is clear that when playing the Nimzo, although there are some lines where he can preserve it, generally Black must be prepared, if necessary, to give up his dark-squared bishop for the c3-knight.

5 b2xc3 *(136)*

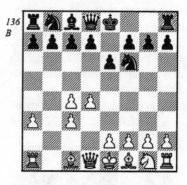

White now has an isolated a-pawn and doubled c-pawns. Nevertheless he has a reasonable centre and, if given the chance, will play f2-f3 and e2-e4. Black may prevent this with ...d7-d5 and ...c7-c5 (hoping to exploit White's c-pawn weaknesses) or with the immediate 5...♘f6-e4. This doesn't actually threaten 6...♘e4xc3 in view of 7 ♕d1-c2, but it does make 6 f2-f3 unplayable in view of 6...♕d8-h4+ 7 g2-g3 ♘e4xg3.

Approaching things from a different angle, Black may allow White to get his pawn to e4, but then try to block things up (making life better for his knights than White's bishops) with ...d7-d6 and ...e7-e5. Naturally, to avoid giving Black outposts such as c5, and to appease his bishops, White is advised as far as possible to keep his pawn structure flexible.

B: 4 f2-f3

Similar to 'A', only here White immediately strives for e2-e4 without putting the question to Black's bishop.

4 ...   d7-d5

The only real alternatives are the challenging 4...c7-c5 and the rather cheeky 4...♘f6-h5 (threatening 5...♕d8-h4+). This text move gives the position the look of a QGD. The b4-bishop is misplaced, but to counter-balance this, there is a hole on e3 and a natural square for the g1-knight has been removed.

5 a2-a3 *(137)*

Now after 5...♗b4xc3+ 6 b2xc3 c7-c5 play has transposed to a Sämisch, but here Black could, if so desired, preserve his bishop.

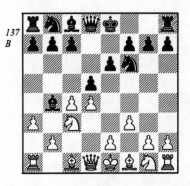

After the retreat, 5...♗b4-e7, White gets 6 e2-e4 in, but 6...d5xe4 7 f3xe4 e6-e5! (staking a claim) is not so straightforward.

C: 4 ♗c1-g5

The 'Leningrad Variation' meets a pin with a pin.

4 ...   h7-h6 *(138)*

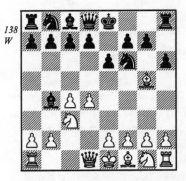

This time it is White who must make a decision although with 4...c7-c5 available (possibly intending to unpin with ...♕d8-a5 and then maybe pile the pressure on the c3-knight with ...♘f6-e4), this question doesn't have to be asked.

5 ♗g5-h4

The only real option as after 5
♗g5xf6, simply 5...♗b4xc3+ 6
b2xc3 ♕d8xf6 (intending ...d7-d6
and ...e6-e5) leaves Black with the
superior pawn structure, whilst
there is little action to be had for
the white rook(s) on the half-open
b-file.

5 ...   c7-c5
6 d7-d5

6 e2-e3 receives the 6...♕d8-a5
unpinning treatment. The text
means that if now 6...♕d8-a5?!,
then 7 ♗h4xf6 leaves the f6-
bishop covering c3. Generally a
wrecking of Black's kingside
pawns will prove more fatal than
a shattering of White's queenside.

6 ...   d7-d6
7 e2-e3

White loses a pawn after 7 e2-e4
g7-g5 8 ♗h4-g3 ♘f6xe4.

7 ...   ♗b4xc3+
8 b2xc3   e7-e5

Black may choose to unpin his
f6-knight with ...g7-g5, but if this
is considered too weakening, then
there is always ...♘b8-d7-f8-g6! If
Black can keep the position
blocked then his position is preferable.

D: 4 g2-g3 *(139)*

Not very common, although I
must confess that this is what I
often play. White fianchettoes his
bishop so as to exert some pressure
on Black's queenside.

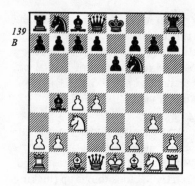

139
B

Black's possibilities include
turning the position into some sort
of 'Catalan' with 4...d7-d5, trying
to block things up with a later ...d7-
d6 and e6-e5 (after, say,
4...♗b4xc3+ 5 b2xc3 0-0) or attacking White's centre with 4...c7-
c5 (or 4...0-0 first).

E: 4 e2-e3   b7-b6 *(140)*

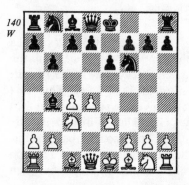

140
W

Black logically seeks to control
the e4-square with a queenside fianchetto. Instead of this Black
could rely on the ...d7-d5 and ...c7-
c5 counter-thrusts, before or after

...0-0. Note that 4...d7-d5 leads to
a QGD type of position, the difference being that Black's bishop
is needlessly on b4 and White's
own dark-squared bishop locked
inside his pawn chain. Black
should be especially careful
when considering ...d7-d5 with
the unlikely pairing of ...b7-b6 in
view of the often embarrassing
♕d1-a4+.

5 ♗f1-d3
Reinforcing the c3-knight with 5
♘g1-e2 looks odd, but is in fact
not silly. This knight would then
be in the way somewhat and since
it would be happy to replace knight
on c3, Black may try to keep his
dark-squared bishop on the board
now (i.e. perhaps retreating it to e7
when attacked).

5 ...   ♗c8-b7
6 ♘g1-f3   ♘f6-e4
Putting a piece here prevents
White's e-pawn advancing!

7 ♕d1-c2   f7-f5
Less logical is ...d7-d5. Black
then gains nothing by doubling
White's pawns (with ....♗b4xc3)
as White will have c4xd5 and then
c3-c4 (opening the position for his
two bishops). In addition the text
move doesn't obstruct the b7-
bishop and potentially enables
Black's major pieces to come into
the game.

8 0-0   ♗b4xc3
9 b2xc3   0-0 (141)
Given time, Black should develop with ...d7-d6 and ...♘b8-d7

and maybe brew up an attack with
...♖f8-f6-h6 and ...♕d8-e8-h5.

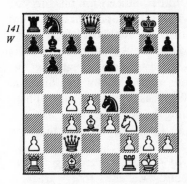

141
W

White should be making plans to
try to eject the black knight from
e4 with either 10 ♘f3-d2 or 10
♘f3-e1 (intending 11 f2-f3).

F: 4 ♕d1-c2 (142)

142
B

At the time of writing this book,
this move (the 'Classical' variation) is the most popular response
to the Nimzo-Indian in top-level
chess. Although White moves his
queen quite early, it is safe here
and it fulfils the purpose of pre-

venting his pawns being doubled. Although (as we will see in 'I') White could perform this function with his c1-bishop, he in fact has other ideas for his bishop, which of course (unlike the queen) has no reservations about venturing further afield. From the diagram Black has three main ways of handling the position:

a) 4...d7-d5, switching to a kind of QGD mode.

b) 4...c7-c5, attacking the recently weakened (by 4 ♕d1-c2) d4-square. 5 d4xc5 ♘b8-a6 or 5...♗b4xc5 when not 6 ♗c1-g5? because of 6...♗c5xf2+! 7 ♔e1xf2 ♘f6-g4+ and 8...♕d8xg5.

c) 4...0-0, the most flexible (though not necessarily best), counting on the fact that 5 e2-e4 is premature here due to 5...d7-d5!. White's whole idea in the Classical is to gain the bishop for the knight without weakening his pawns and so 5 a2-a3 is usual, whereupon 5...♗b4xc3 6 ♕c2xc3 b7-b6 sees Black returning to the theme of controlling e4.

G: 4 ♕d1-b3

White's aims here are the same as after 4 ♕d1-c2 but he hopes to avoid the tempo loss of a2-a3. Probably Black's best move here is 4...c7-c5, but an interesting trick to note comes after 4...a7-a5 5 ♘g1-f3 (the reader should observe how this might also arise from 'H') 5...b7-b6 6 a2-a3 *(143)*.

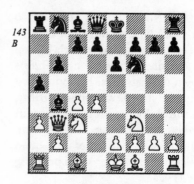

6...a5-a4! and if 7 ♕b3xb4, then 7...♘b8-c6 8 ♕b4-b5 ♖a8-a5 and the white queen is lost. Hence White must retreat with 7 ♕b3-c2 when after 7...♗b4xc3+ 8 ♕c2xc3, Black will have managed to fix White's queenside (due to the *en passant* rule) with ...a5-a4 for free (normally White tries to prevent this with b2-b3).

H: 4 ♘g1-f3

A sensible move which could quite easily transpose into other variations.

4 ...   b7-b6

Staying with the queenside fianchetto theme. However, simply 4...0-0 and 4...c7-c5 deserve a lot of attention, probably White's best against the latter being 5 g2-g3 as in 'D'.

5 ♗c1-g5

The difference between this and the Leningrad Variation ('C') is that the black queen will not make it to a5 now, but White has committed a knight to f3. However, if White had known a fianchetto was coming, he might have preferred f2-f3 intending e2-e4, but on the other hand Black wouldn't then have fianchettoed!

    5 ...   **♝c8-b7**
    6 e2-e3

For the time being White contents himself with advancing his e-pawn just one square.

    6 ...   **h7-h6**
    7 ♝g5-h4 *(144)*

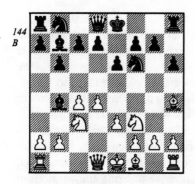

144
B

Now Black must decide whether to go on the offensive with 7...g7-g5 8 ♝h4-g3 ♞f6-e4, exerting pressure on the white c3-knight. As this weakens his kingside, he may opt for the more solid 7...♝b4xc3+ 8 b2xc3 d7-d6. As I once find out to my cost, the natural 9 ♝f1-d3 intending 10 0-0 is then too passive. Instead White should immediately test Black with 9 ♞f3-d2 (planning f2-f3 and e2-e4 to blunt the diagonal).

I: **4 ♝c1-d2**

The natural novice reaction, although practically never seen at top level. White prevents his pawns from being doubled and unpins his knight. However in the Nimzo-Indian it is clear that Black is only too happy to concede a bishop for a knight if it means him gaining control of the key e4-square (as he will do here).

    4 ...   **0-0**

4...d7-d5 would also be perfectly acceptable, but probably not 4...b7-b6?! in view of 5 f2-f3!.

    5 a2-a3   **♝b4xc3**
    6 ♝d2xc3   **♞f6-e4** *(145)*

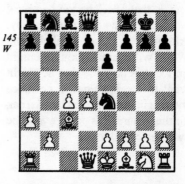

145
W

It is fairly clear now that, if Black so desires, he will be able to trade his knight for White's bishop anyhow. Nonetheless Black will be more interested in keeping it posted on the excellent e4-square and will be prepared to bolster it with ...f7-f5. Then, as we have seen before, the black queen and rook(s) can zoom out to attack White's kingside. Black can solve his queenside development problems with ...d7-d6 and possibly even ...e6-e5. The b8-knight will move to d7 and a queenside fianchetto is also available, as f2-f3 is not possible in view of ...♕d8-h4+.

33) The Benoni

| 1 d2-d4 | ♘g8-f6 |
| 2 c2-c4 | |

Again we see White playing this space-gaining move that is associated with 'main line' queen's pawn openings. 2 ♘g1-f3 is of course very sensible, but the problem is that Black is yet to reveal which defence he is going to play. Although it is not unlikely that White will want his king's knight on f3, it is possible that he might want to use his f-pawn, i.e. once the knight is on f3, the f2-pawn can neither share this square nor be swerved round to f4!

| 2 ... | c7-c5 *(146)* |

146
W

Black immediately strikes out in the centre and is not worried about

3 d4xc5. Just like in the Queen's Gambit, this pawn can be rounded up, here with 3...e7-e6 and 3...♘b8-a6 being likely candidates.

3 d4-d5

The most natural and aggressive move. White encroaches upon Black's territory. Also playable are the more cautious 3 ♘g1-f3 and the slightly passive 3 e2-e3.

3 ...   e7-e6

This move heralds the beginning of an imbalancing process from which a kingside versus queenside majority battle is formed. Having used a couple of moves to get his pawn to d5, White will not want to play 4 d5xe6? f7xe6 when with ...d7-d5 on the cards, Black will soon have a nice centre to complement his useful half-open f-file. Likewise utilizing the *en passant* rule after 3...e7-e5 in the already seen 'Czech Benoni' would be a poor choice.

A popular alternative for today's attacking club player is the 'Benko Gambit', 3...b7-b5. A typical continuation highlighting Black's aims is 4 c4xb5 a7-a6 5 e2-e3 g7-g6 6 ♘b1-c3 ♗f8-g7 7 ♘g1-f3 0-0 8 b5xa6 d7-d6 *(147)*. Black obviously has no problems regaining the a6-pawn. That still leaves him one pawn down, but the point of the gambit is that Black uses the half-open a- and b-files with his major pieces to exert pressure on White's queenside.

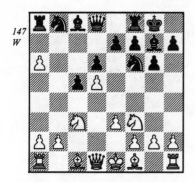

147
W

His fianchettoed bishop also looks menacing and when the light-squared bishops are exchanged, even the black knights may get in on the act if ...c5-c4 is achieved and a trusty steed can get to c5 and then to d3. Black has a very solid pawn structure and if he is able to win back one of White's pawns, then he is favourite to win.

    4 ♘b1-c3   e6xd5
    5 c4xd5   d7-d6 *(148)*

Things could get very unpleasant for Black if White were able to put and then keep his own pawn on d6.

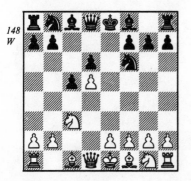

148
W

We have arrived at the main starting position of what, strictly speaking, is the 'Modern Benoni'. Black's next few moves are predictable. A kingside fianchetto is intended and after castling, Black may try to hinder any central tricks by White by placing his rook on the half-open e-file. No doubt given half a chance, we would see Black's queenside pawns motor down the board as well. Hence the ball is in White's court. He must similarly decide on a piece and pawn formation which will hopefully help him to progress whilst stifling Black's play. Indeed theory provides White with many possible set-ups – a selection which surprisingly includes a kingside fianchetto of his own. Possibly more appealing though is:

    6 e2-e4   g7-g6
    7 f2-f4

Probably the most threatening move, as it would appear that with this f-pawn in a supporting role, White's e-pawn will be more dangerous than Black's equivalent c-pawn. Nevertheless White has alternatives in 7 ♘g1-f3 (with 8 ♗f1-d3 or 8 ♗f1-e2 in mind) or 7 ♗f1-d3 (with 8 ♘g1-e2 in mind).

    8 ♗f1-b5+!

Sticking to the 'rules' White should play 8 ♘g1-f3, but this inspirational check momentarily puts Black in a tangle. Whilst there are many complications, the point is that after 8...♗c8-d7 or 8...♘b8-d7, White has 9 e4-e5 when Black's minor pieces are running out of room.

8 ...   ♘f6-d7

Not a desirable move to have to play.

9 a2-a4!

Another key move. White renders it very difficult for Black to utilize his queenside pawn majority as ...b7-b5 is going to be impossible for quite a while.

9 ...   0-0
10 ♘g1-f3 *(149)*

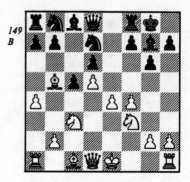

149
B

With more freedom for his pieces, White is generally considered to have a comfortable advantage. However, there is always the danger that he may overreach, when having far-advanced pawns may backfire.

Index of Openings

Numbers refer to page numbers. A page number in **bold** indicates that there is a section devoted to this opening.